twentysomething

Life Beyond College

Denny Rydberg

ZondervanPublishingHouse

Grand Rapids, Michigan

A Division of HarperCollins*Publishers*

Published by Zondervan Publishing House
1415 Lake Drive, S.E., Grand Rapids, Michigan 49506

Library of Congress Cataloging-in-Publication Data

Rydberg, Denny
    Twentysomething : life beyond college / Denny Rydberg.
      p. cm.
    ISBN 0-310-53571-9
    1. Young adults—Religious life. 2. Christian life—1960–
3. College graduates—United States—Religious life. I. Title.
II. Title: Twenty something.
BV4850.R93   1991
248.8'4—dc20   90–22143
                                         CIP

Edited by Lori J. Walburg

Printed in the United States of America

91 92 93 94 95 96 / CH / 10 9 8 7 6 5 4 3 2 1

To my son Jeremy,
who in twelve short years
will be twentysomething.

CONTENTS

CHAPTER 1

In the Beginning

You've probably heard of the popular television show, *thirtysomething*. The show portrays the struggles and growing pains of baby boomers, adults in their thirties: their relationships, their careers, their marriages, their lifestyles. You may have watched the show while you were in college and wondered if life outside of college was actually like that. But you didn't know. All the college graduates you might have asked have moved on. You have little idea of what they're doing, what their life is like. Life in the twenties beyond college seems as foreign and unimaginable as life as an outcast in Bangladesh.

Twentysomething has been written to give you a glimpse of life beyond college. Let me say from the start, a twentysomething is not the same as a thirtysomething. You face different challenges, different problems, in your twenties. But you're not heading into those challenges without some advantages.

If you've just graduated from college, you're among the brightest and best of the twentysomethings. You have years of education and experience under your belt. You've faced the pressures of time, papers, tests, and schedules in college. You have related to peers, older adults, and children.

You've also proven yourself in other areas. You've held down part-time jobs. You've won scholarships.

7

You've competed against the best of your peers physically, mentally, or artistically. You've volunteered your time in student government or neighborhood work or college publications.

Along the way you've also been involved in significant relationships. You've made close friends with members of the opposite and same sex. Some of you have fallen in love. Others haven't. Some are married or thinking about marriage. Some are not.

But the point is: you didn't just fall off a turnip truck. As a twentysomething, you've got some savvy. Some smarts. Some confidence.

You're out of college (or almost out) and you're ready to charge ahead. But you know there may be a few pitfalls out there, and you'd like to avoid tumbling headfirst into them. You want to maximize your potential and live life to the full.

With these facts in mind, I've written this book for you, the twentysomething person. This isn't a textbook *about* twentysomethings, though we will look at some developmental tasks that are unique to your age. It's a book written *to* twentysomethings to help you understand what life is like beyond college. And which of us wouldn't like a chance to peek into the future to see what's out there, what we're up against?

To help you gaze into your future, I've included some thoughts from people who are either in their twenties right now or still have some good ideas about what being twentysomething is all about. They should know better than anyone just what you're getting into after college.

So, brightest and best of the twentysomethings, may you profit from this book.

CHAPTER 2
Life Is Untidy

I graduated from college with honors and a good résumé. I had plans.

The Vietnam War was in full swing and I knew that along with my fellow graduates, I could be drafted very quickly into the Army and, as a draftee, not have much of a choice as to how I would spend my time. So I decided to take the Air Force officer placement tests and serve my time with some degree of choice. That was controlling my own destiny, I thought.

I took the physical along with dozens of other guys. We marched in our shorts from one room to another, coughing here, having our blood pressure taken there, opening our mouths, sticking out our tongues, and doing all the things you do in a "mass physical."

Then I sat in a room and took mental and aptitudinal tests for what seemed like hours. I would receive my appointment, serve my country, travel some, maybe even further my formal education while in the service (all at Uncle Sam's expense), and then move on.

To what, I wasn't sure. Maybe graduate school to become a psychologist. Psychology had been my college major. Or maybe coaching. Or perhaps the ministry (I had been a church youth director while in college). But step one, the Air Force, sounded like a good step to me.

So what happened?

Nothing. I didn't hear one word from the government. So I graduated in June and took the first temporary job I could find. I drove a bus full of strawberry pickers from my hometown to Sakuma Brothers Farm and acted as a field boss once we got there, "helping" kids pick berries.

The berry season was over and still no word from the Force. So I took "temporary" job number two: common laborer for Plant Maintenance, a company that provided workers at the oil refineries near my hometown. I dug holes, cleaned scummy oil tanks, tarred a reservoir, and did whatever the oil company needed. I even got a promotion to "Painter's Helper" before running an electric buffer into my knee. Sixteen stitches later, I learned what it was like to draw workmen's compensation for the first and only time in my life.

But still no word from my friends in the Air Force. Instead of seeing the world, I was getting closer to home the longer I was away from college. And I was using none of the skills I had honed during my university career.

When the summer ended and my plans had not materialized in the way I had hoped, I made a quick call to the head of the department of psychology at my alma mater and said, "Help, I need someplace to go. Can you find me a scholarship somewhere to grad school? Can you give me some leads?" A day later I had a teaching assistantship at a nearby university. Full ride. The only problem: I had never talked to anyone on the faculty of that university's psychology department. I had not even looked at their college catalog! I just headed up there on the day before classes. It was a chancy way to choose a graduate school. And I paid the price.

I went there to get an M.A. in psychology and

discovered it was not for me. I did well academically, but it was a school that focused on behavioral psychology, and I didn't. I was reading articles on the "Echo Location of Flying Insects by Bats" and other such tomes that were as far away from what I thought psychology to be as Mother Teresa is from Attila the Hun.

So at the end of the quarter, I walked into the office of the head of the school of psychology at my new university and said, "Thanks for the scholarship. I've appreciated all you've done for me this quarter, but I think there are others who would appreciate this scholarship more than I would." And I left.

Over six months had passed since graduation day, and the road I'd taken was a lot different from that which I'd planned. Life beyond college was not as I'd anticipated.

In one of her books Elisabeth Elliot wrote, "Life is untidy." That was a perfect description of what I had discovered in just a few months out of college.

You may be where I was: out of college and discovering the untidiness of life. Or you may be on the verge of graduating and wonder what to expect.

This book is designed to help you regardless of whether you're out of or in college. I want you to get a handle on what to expect and some hints on what to do once you move beyond college. And, as I said in chapter 1, I'm not writing this from my own experience only. As a person who spends most of his time with college students and recent graduates, I've been able to recruit some people in their twenties to lend their insights into the life of the twentysomething.

One contributor to this book is Mike Neelley. Mike graduated from the University of Washington in 1985 with a B.A. in English Literature. When I talked with him about life in the twenties, he said, "Our society implies that we are to know who we are, what we want, and where we are going by the time we graduate from college. However, our educational institutions do little, if anything, to prepare us for this. At most, they prepare us to interview for a career. So, we are faced, for possibly the first time, with questions of life and identity, and we no longer have the communities of family, school, or church in the same way we had them in the past. Still, it is precisely the way we have had them in the past, consciously or unconsciously, that sets the stage for interactions and expectations."

In other words, we are not as well prepared for what we will face after college as we may have thought. The reason for that ill-preparedness, as we'll see in the next chapter, is pretty obvious.

CHAPTER 3

There Is a Difference

Let's admit it right away: there is a vast difference between the college world and the non-college world. If you're already "out there," you know the truth of this statement. If you're not, trust me. And trust the others who have contributed to this book.

Tough Questions

Pete Shimer, a Certified Public Accountant in his late twenties, says, "Many people think the toughest transition in life is from high school to college. Being away from home for the first time can be extremely difficult and lonely. However, I think the first two to five years after college are the most difficult. You ask the tough questions: Will I ever find a job? How do I meet people outside of work and bars? Will I ever get married? Do I even have time for a relationship? What's happened to all my friends now that they're married and I'm not? How will I ever be able to afford a house? Do I really need life insurance and, if so, what type?

"The post-college adventure brings these questions and many more. The biggest difference, for me, between college and adulthood is *not* that new experiences take place in my life. The difference is that there are a lot less people to share the ups and downs with. In college, you are surrounded by a very homogeneous group of people. You all live the same experiences, like getting shut out of a class you need for graduation or getting a poor grade on a final. There are plenty of people to commiserate with you. They are in the same boat with you at the same time. Not so in the world beyond college. Everyone's not in the same boat, and some that are don't care that much about how you're doing."

Social Changes

Doug Early, who's a couple of years younger than Pete, agrees with Pete that the social differences after college are a key adjustment you have to make. Doug says, "The greatest difference in life after college is social. Time management, finances, knowing what to do—none of these was easy for me, and they haven't gotten much better. But the greatest difference for me has been in the social area of my life. For the most part, your social life is built into college structurally. After college, people have the better portion of most of their days committed to work. Because you're so busy working and don't see the people you most care about on a daily basis like you may have in college, you spend more time and energy trying to *find time* for people you really care about. In college, you are surrounded by people your own age—in classes, at meals, in the library, in living situations. In the outside world, those people are still around but so are hundreds of others of all ages and backgrounds that absorb the people you're looking for."

Relationship Changes

Two more friends, Stu and Sue Harris, married for two years and now teaching English in Japan, made relationships their theme in talking about the differences between college and beyond. "You go from college with roommates and 'full-time' companions sharing all of your secrets, thoughts, and dreams, to post-college, where you're now not together as much. You and your friends now have even more demands on your time and energy. And to make matters more complex, sometimes you are going in different directions from your old college buddies. How you keep 'changing friendships' strong was one of our biggest dilemmas after college."

Single to Married

"Going from single to being married is also a big adjustment," says Sue. "Instead of sharing everything on my mind with my girlfriend, I was now sharing it with my husband and wondering how much of what I shared with my husband I could share with my girlfriend. This was hard for me. Also most single friends assumed a married friend spends every moment with her spouse, so they stopped inviting me to do things! I started feeling isolated. That was different from college."

Parental Changes

In addition, your relationship with your parents continues to change. Even in college, your parents may have played the "supportive, parental role." Paying for your college education. Making those car insurance premiums. Sending care packages. Checking with you on your grades. For most graduates, the child/parent relationship changes. Parents of college graduates start to pull away the economic umbilical cord, and some students even feel that the safety net ("well, if I really get into trouble, the folks will rescue me") has been removed. Most parents finally realize that their child is an adult (although they still may treat their graduate as a child at times) after college graduation, but especially when that child marries. "You're on your own, kid" is the general feeling after a marriage. And that's a change many people in their twenties experience.

Hours and Lifestyle

Normal living hours change as well. You can't skip work in the same way you might have blown off an 8:30 A.M. class. And that means you probably have to be more disciplined in what time you go to bed. Living situations change. If you lived in a fraternity or sorority or in a dorm, meals were prepared for you. Not anymore. You have to become more disciplined in the area of meal preparation or eat less food or become a junk food junkie or spend all your money eating out.

Finding a fellowship group in a church can be difficult, too, if you've just moved to a new area after college. And some "young adult" groups may not seem as lively or as warm to you after the homogeneous college group with whom you spent time in college.

Money and Success

Materialism becomes a bigger issue after college too. Either possessing things or envying those who do causes problems. Questions of success emerge in your twenties. What is success and how can you measure it when the world might measure it in another way? If you're teaching school to a bunch of squirrelly third graders, pulling down $18,000 a year and driving a used Toyota, and your former college roommate is making a cool $75,000 in investment banking and tooling around in a new BMW, who's the most successful? And before you come to a quick conclusion, who's to say the guy in the three-piece suit is *less* successful in God's sight just because he drives a *better* car than you? And if that guy is just as successful in God's sight, then why not quit your teaching job and go for the bucks?

Questions. Issues. Changes. Demands. It's a jungle out there. But it's also an adventure that's worth the price of the ride.

CHAPTER 4

It Comes with the Territory

"When I was a child, I talked liked a child, I thought like a child, I reasoned like a child. When I became a man, I put childish ways behind me" (1 Corinthians 13:11).

In this, one of his most famous statements, the apostle Paul revealed his grasp of the fundamental premise of developmental psychology.

Developmental psychology studies the development and maturation of the human person. It recognizes that your tasks at the age of three are different from your tasks at the age of twenty-three. A developmental psychologist—not to mention life itself—will tell us that people in their twenties face tasks unique to their age. For you to continue to grow and mature, you need to accomplish these specific tasks.

As I told you in the previous chapters, my friends and I are writing a book *to* you about how to successfully negotiate life beyond college. We're not writing a book *about* twentysomething people. *To* and *about* are very different things.

However, in writing *to* you I occasionally need to address some things *about* you. And that's the case in this chapter. For you to move beyond college it's helpful to know what developmental tasks are unique to people in their twenties. Therefore I've asked my friend Doug Hansen, a licensed therapist, for help in explaining those tasks. In the remainder of this chapter you'll discover the tasks that "come with the territory" of being in your twenties—along with some ideas on how best to accomplish them.

Pushing Away from the Dock

One of the most critical tasks you face in your twenties is to achieve greater independence from those who have parented you in the past. This is necessary to establish your own independence and identity.

Doug Hansen says, "The interpersonal and intellectual experience of life in the university is full of adjustments to new people and new ideas. The college student is often sad to see those exciting days come to an end, but he may also be relieved that the 'training' is over and that the hectic pace of academia will be replaced with a peaceful sense of a settled, predictable life. While such expectations are understandable, the post-college person in his twenties now faces more profound transitions than the changes experienced during the college years. The academic institution functions *in loco parentis*. Therefore the process of leaving the 'home' of the collegiate environment marks the birth of adulthood. Out of college, the twenties person seeks to define himself in the world."

In other words, your job as you move through life is to establish a separate self, a person different from your parents, an independent adult with his or her own identity. You may think you had established that identity in college. However, whether you realized it or not, the university has functioned like a parent, making it difficult for you to fully achieve this task. But now that you are moving beyond college, you can work at this task. You now have an opportunity (probably for the first time) to define yourself in the world.

So although some of the demands of college life will abate—the hectic pace of mid-terms, finals, endless papers, deadlines, demands, and the busy social scene of college—life will not become all that tranquil. For you have some important, sometimes stressful work to do. The years of the twenties stand before you full of many more significant transitions and tasks than you ever experienced in college.

The truth is that this "pushing away from the dock" (a term coined by author Sharon Parks)—the task of achieving independence and leaving the nest of home or college—is a *process*, not an *event*. Although you may have left home at eighteen, you may have been financially or emotionally dependent on your parents. Now you've graduated from college and some of the ropes or ties to your parents have been cut with the graduation ceremony. But there are still plenty of lines left on your boat. Some will fray away through the years. Some will be cut quickly by you. And, at other times, more ropes will be added by you or your parents that will have to be cut before you can successfully push away.

To compound the situation, some parents will have more difficulty than others realizing that the goal of child rearing is to produce a loved, capable, independent adult—a person free to leave the dock with the blessing of his or her parents. This maturation process is biblical. The Bible says, "Therefore a man *leaves* his father and mother and *cleaves* to his wife" (Genesis 2:24 RSV). Leaving needs to take place before cleaving (intimacy) can occur. And this leaving will be a process

21

that begins and continues well before engagement or marriage (cleaving) ever takes place.

This leaving the nest—this pushing away from the dock—can be difficult even for those people from stable, loving families who have little to "rebel" against. In fact, people from stable homes may try to "foul the nest" with sudden irritations or differences of opinion that create almost artificial difficulties to help them leave a soft, warm place for the great unknown.

In working with students over the years, I'm struck by the fact that students from more solid homes (in contrast to more dysfunctional homes) realize in their college years how good they had it growing up as they are exposed to the homes (or stories about the homes) of their classmates. These students obviously feel grateful to their parents, and sometimes they develop an obsessive need to live up to their parents' wishes and desires in order to reward these "great parents." The result is that instead of pushing away, they add a few ropes in their "people pleasing/parent pleasing" mode that they carry with them into their twenties. So for both twentysomething people from solid homes and for those from homes that were more shaky, the task is complex.

And then there are some individuals in their twenties who make new discoveries. Jim Allen, a coworker of mine, observed this about families: "What you thought was the Brady Bunch now seems more like the Munsters. The truth probably lies somewhere in between. In my twenties, my search for 'myself' has led me to try to understand my family. In a culture that pushes rugged individualism and independence and teaches we are responsible for what we do and who we are, I've realized that I can't understand myself or anyone else just by looking at them as individuals. I need to understand where they came from. I am an individual personality with a unique genetic makeup, but I have been significantly influenced by my family and the environment we shared."

You can't always tell how well people are doing in this task of establishing an independent identity because what appears on the outside may not mirror what is going on inside that person. For instance, those from homes where significant needs have not been met sometimes consciously or subconsciously remain in the "child" role in hopes that their mother or father may "change" and "give them" what they always needed. These same people may outwardly appear very independent while on the inside long to remain emotionally dependent on that which was not sufficiently nurturing in childhood.

When the ropes of a dysfunctional home or the ropes of trying too hard to please "perfect parents" are wrapped around the boat, pushing away from the dock can be difficult. Others remain tied to the dock because they feel they must care for or shepherd their parents. This problem has been called co-dependency.

But regardless of the ropes, pushing away from the dock is a process. This process is fueled by the energy and wonderful idealism of those in their twenties and the emergence of a new, separate identity eager to express itself.

Exploring Places Unknown

Doug Hansen says, "According to Robert Kegan, a founder of 'constructive-developmental' theory, the twenties person is moving from being understood or known to themselves by the nature of their relationships to more of a sense of self-authorship. The forces which shape the self are becoming more internal than external. Ambition and achievement take immediacy over affiliation and affection. The self 'seals up' as jobs become careers and helpmates become life partners."

In other words, a task for persons in their twenties is to move from being defined by relationships to being defined more by self. Personal ambition and personal achievement demand greater expression.

In theory, the childhood need for "love and belonging" launches the ambition and achievement drives of the twenties. Fueled by the grueling years of academic preparation to "do something," the college grad wants to do just that. But the idealism that forges the graduates' courage and vision also complicates and frustrates the life of graduates when they confront the realities of life. The emerging graduates find the job market a tough place in which to land. Prepared for a "career," they may find themselves working eight to ten hours a day merely at a job, not a career. Such a position is frustrating when you're ambitious and achievement oriented.

In facing this particular developmental task, it's important to remember that

1. *You are not wasting your time.* The job you have may not be ideal, but at least it's paying your bills, giving you experience, and helping you to decide where your skills lie. The time of testing the waters vocationally is not a waste.

2. *Both your talents and the job market take time and space to investigate.* Think of your career in terms of a *process.* A career path is not like a train that you have to be on by 5 A.M., but more like a car you drive yourself, taking detours, enjoying scenic routes, and experiencing delays before you ultimately reach your destination.

3. *You will need a network of support during these years.*

These initial months and years of self-identification and exploration require a lot of energy, physically and emotionally. Save some of that energy to build and maintain old friendships worth keeping.

The Urge to Merge

In addition to the task of self-authorship and realizing personal ambition and achievement, there is another drive at work, another task to face. This is the need to establish intimacy. What an ironic situation: the dual and apparently conflicting drives of independence and intimacy are alive and well in the same person at the same time. You have just left the nest of parents and university and now, at the dawn of this drive to achieve and express the newfound self and freedom, you find yourself also yearning to establish a new intimacy in relationships, an intimacy that is committed, exclusive, and loyal.

Doug says, "Erik Erikson, the renowned psychoanalyst, presents this stage of growth as one of achieving intimacy versus isolation. Erikson postulates that the successful resolution of the previous stage of development, identity vs. role confusion, which transpires during the later teen years, enables the young adult to acquire capacities for fidelity and devotion. As with any stage, the newly acquired capacities are then tested within the emerging psychological context. Having acquired a sense of identity, the twenties person seeks to join that 'self' to another self, employing the values of fidelity and devotion. The risk lies in losing what one has only recently gained—the sense of identity. The search for intimacy requires that a person be able to maintain that sense of self while building a deep emotional attachment to another's identity."

This is the dilemma: you want to have intimacy with another person, but at the same time you don't want to lose the sense of identity you've been working on during your college years. You left the nest when you graduated. You've been working on who you are and what that means. And now, you're thinking about building your own nest and you've got to figure out how that works—by no means an easy task.

Doug continues, "The ability to be expressive of the self in the close emotional proximity of the other determines the level of intimate satisfaction within the relationship. Failure to be self-expressive in the midst of such closeness means a threat to the existence of the identity. Such a person would then need to refrain from attachments at that deep level. Erikson sees a sense of emotional isolation necessary in such people to protect the existence of their identity. Of course, these concepts exist on a continuum, with varying degrees of successful resolution for each individual.

"Because intimate relations between the sexes carry feelings of competitiveness and hate in addition to affection and love, the twenties person is faced with the challenge of exercising fidelity and devotion to protect the goodness of the same relationship that he or she may want to destroy."

In the eighties, many young adults postponed marriage until their mid-twenties or early thirties until they could achieve more schooling or establish their careers. Such a move can be beneficial in that it allows more time for personal maturity and career expression. But it can also be laden with liabilities. Upon leaving the "groupness" of the early twenties, it may be more difficult to meet potential marriage partners. The demands of the workplace tend to push you more toward isolation than toward community. It takes more work to find friends and people you would like to date. Most likely it will take more effort on your part to initiate and maintain the relationships that are crucial for emotional support.

In the next chapter on relationships, some practical helps on developing and maintaining friendships are given but for now, here are some suggestions:

1. *Seek out groups that express your interests and fill your needs.* Join a church choir, a volleyball team, a book group—places where you can meet people and get to know them in an informal setting.

2. *Schedule time and save energy to maintain friendships and to date and entertain.* Outside of college, a social life doesn't just come to you. You have to make more of an effort to plan your social activities.

3. *Get to know people very different from yourself.* It is important to keep a fairly broad base of emotional support. Sometimes in our need to establish intimacy, we put too much burden on too few friends. We all need family, acquaintances, coworkers, and casual friends, as well as intimate friends, to stay healthy.

It is out of a healthy sense of self that we can extend ourselves to many in relationships, to a few in friendships, and to one in marriage.

Developing Your Own Faith

James Fowler, the faith development theorist, has studied the twentysomething person's approach to faith. To Fowler, the person entering the twenties is able to synthesize the experiences and truth of how they know God and themselves. This understanding is highly influenced by the interpersonal relationships and judgments of the significant others in a person's life. Negative factors, such as disillusionment with trusted leaders or a change in doctrine, can contribute to the breakdown of this conventional picture. When this happens, individuals are forced to a critical examination of their beliefs and how they were formed.

The task for you in your twenties is to assume responsibility for which beliefs you want to embrace and to fashion a lifestyle that is uniquely suited to your personal understanding of self and God.

In summary, here's what you can expect to come with the territory of the twenties:

1. *Get ready for change and transition.* Life ain't easy anywhere, but it doesn't get less complicated or less tidy in the twenties.

2. *Your relationship with your parents will change.* To establish your own identity you will need to become more aware of how your family has shaped you at the same time that you differentiate yourself from them.

3. *You will feel a drive to achieve.* As you work to define yourself, you will think more in terms of individual achievement than relationships. You will look for ways to define and prove yourself in your work.

4. *Your desire for intimacy will grow.* With your newly found capacity for committed love, you will seek someone with whom to share that love. However, you will need to balance the desire for intimacy with your need for independence and identity.

5. *You will define your faith on your own terms.* Faith will work less in terms of externals that others impose on you and more in terms of internals as you work out for yourself what your faith means to you.

At every stage in life we have some developmental tasks. Infants need to learn to eat and to recognize their parents. Toddlers need to learn how to walk and use the bathroom in socially accepted ways. Preschoolers need some social skills. Elementary children need to learn to read, process information, make judgments. Adolescents need to survive all the changes and demands of puberty. College-age people work at identity as well as term papers. And you in your twenties have your tasks as well.

Living in the midst of these tasks is tricky. And this "tricky living" is the subject of the rest of this book. We'll begin with the trickiest area of all—relationships.

CHAPTER 5

Changing Relationships: The Art of Silver and Gold

When I was a child, I learned a song that went something like this: "Make new friends but keep the old; one is silver, the other gold."

I like the idea expressed in that song, but frankly, keeping old friends is not always possible, for several reasons. One is the sheer weight of all those friendships on life. If you keep adding new friendships and never let some of the old ones go, you'll spend all your time just trying to stay in contact and be a good friend "to everyone." The other reason is that life simply doesn't allow you to keep all old friends. Old friends move, change interests, and grow apart for legitimate reasons.

So I'd like to edit the childhood song, "Make a *few* new friends but keep a *few* old; one is silver, the other gold."

My assumption in this chapter is that you know about making and keeping friendships. You know about letting go. After all, not all your high-school buddies were your best friends in college. However, you may still have some great friendships that "survived" junior high, high school, and college. And you rightfully cherish those relationships.

You don't need a course in Friendship 101. You could write the book and teach the class yourself. But, as has been said before, relationships and the development of relationships change once you move beyond college. Many people go from being surrounded by many people their own age, with easy access to them in college through sororities, fraternities, church, sports teams, and dorms, to a situation where they don't have much contact or easy access to people their own age.

In chapter 3, Pete Shimer, Doug Early, and Stu and Sue Harris all mentioned the changing nature of relationships in our twenties: how they change, how they must be maintained, how they influence the other aspects of our lives.

And, in the last chapter, it was clear that relational issues are crucial to people in their twenties from a developmental standpoint. The move toward greater intimacy, the search for identity, the pushing away from the dock—all involve relationships.

So let's look at the new dynamics of relational living. Whether you move away from the city where your campus was located or simply move off campus, the search for new, significant relationships is critical.

Moving Away and Making New Friends

Kelly Lunda, a former world-class ice speed skater from Wisconsin, moved to Seattle a few years ago (where "speed skating" is considered something you do on a skateboard). This is what she said. "When I first moved 3,000 miles from Madison to Seattle, I looked forward to working every fifth weekend because it filled my empty weekends. I knew only one person when I moved here. I went from a phone that never stopped ringing to a phone that only rang when it was the wrong number. I went from having so many friends that I couldn't find time to see them all to not knowing anyone.

"So I chose my job carefully. Fortunately, as a physical therapist, I had an option of where to work, so I took a job with a young staff, many of whom were single. Not everyone has this option, but it's something to consider. I knew my friends at work would be my first good contacts.

"I also called the Fellowship of Christian Athletes (an organization with whom I'd been involved in college) within two weeks of arriving. I knew I needed to get into fellowship quickly before my new environment pulled me in many directions. Lucky for me, FCA was very active and had many people involved who were post-college.

"FCA opened a whole new world for me in Seattle. However, again I took the initiative and was consistent in attending weekly meetings. I met some great friends in FCA because I went to nearly all the activities, and I also planned meetings and stuffed envelopes for one of their mailings. I re-discovered the fact that working together helps build relationships. I was also reminded that you rarely develop deep friendships in large groups. Friendships develop in small groups or over time spent one-on-one. You get to know people in proportion to how much time you spend with them. I decided early on not to try to go to a *different* group every night to meet new people. If you do, you'll end up with lots of acquaintances and no friends. And I learned again the advice my mother gave me as a child, 'To have a friend, be a friend.'

"But I did more than FCA. I joined the Mountaineers. I took a basic climbing class, Rock and Glacier Climbing, one night a week for six weeks and went on four field trips. I met people who loved the outdoors and knew the area. They could show me the great places that would have taken ages for me to find on my own.

"These activities kept me busy, challenged me, exhilarated me, opened up a whole new world, and wowed me with some beautiful places."

That's one woman's story. How do you build relationships when you're in a new area? Let's summarize what Kelly said and I'll add a few thoughts of my own.

1. *Remember that developing good friendships takes time.* Your college buddies weren't great friends immediately. You probably had to work to develop those friendships and watch them grow into solid friendships. That same process will need to occur again.

2. *Find places to get involved.* If you move to a new area and know few people, you have to make the first move. Here are some suggestions for things you can do to meet people:

- Take fun classes: sports, cooking, camping, rock climbing, or some community college classes (we're not talking about an advanced degree here; we're talking about meeting people).
- Join a club.
- Check into church activities.
- Call parachurch organizations.
- Call alumni groups; you'd be surprised how much they can help when you relocate.
- Don't be afraid to go to places alone.

● Do things by yourself; it can be fun and you might meet some people along the way.

Keeping the Friends You Already Have

But there's another dynamic to friendships and relationships in the post-college years. That's keeping up with friends you've already made—your buddies on those intramural teams, friends from your residence halls, even old friends from high school who have survived the college years. How do you keep those friendships going in the midst of change? Here are a few suggestions for those situations:

1. *Remember: not all your old friends will remain as close as they have in the past.* As my dad told me one day, "You've got to learn to say good-bye." Dynamics change. Interests differ. Old friends get involved in new relationships and you may not be as close. Don't expect to take all your old friendships with you.

2. *Work at keeping in touch with those friendships you want to keep.* If friends move away, write letters, use the phone, or fax them a message. Or send video or audio cassettes. Bob Thompson, an old college roommate, and I have sent audio cassettes back and forth for over fifteen years, and we've had a good time doing it. It's been one of the major factors in our enduring friendship.

3. *Invest some time and money in visits.* If your friends live out of town, visit. If they live in town, make the effort to see them.

4. *Start a small group.* I know some women who were involved in a small fellowship group while in college. They're married now, but the group is going on. They meet weekly, and their friendship has flourished.

5. *Start a larger group.* A bunch of my former students started a new group that meets in one of their homes. They call it Post College Fellowship (PCF). Original, huh? But it works. They know how difficult it is to find good, healthy, Christian fellowship after college, and they know how tough it is to make the time to see old friends and develop new ones. So they started a weekly group. Over thirty new and old friends gather each week.

That New Living Situation

One aspect of relationships we haven't yet addressed is the situation of roommates and where you're going to live. Because roommates have great potential for joy or sorrow, it's important to decide on the type of person with whom you want to share a house or apartment.

The first step in roommate hunting is to know yourself. Decide what you want. Do you prefer to live alone, with several roommates, or with one roommate? To help you answer that question, let's look at the pros and cons of each living situation.

Pros of Living Alone

1. You have the freedom to choose your own lifestyle. You can choose your own furnishings, keep your place as clean as you want, invite guests over when you like, and make the place your home.

2. You have the time and quiet necessary to accomplish tasks.

3. You don't have to deal with roommate conflicts.

Cons of Living Alone

1. It will be more expensive. Not only are you alone responsible for rent, phone, gas, and electric bills, but you have no one with whom to pool household resources like dishes, furniture, and appliances.

2. It can be isolating. You will need to put out more effort to meet, call, and see friends.

Pros of Living with Several Roommates

1. You'll find it easier to get involved in outside activities because something is always happening. You will hear about more parties, events, and outings because your network of "who knows whom" is larger.

2. You can get to know different people and are exposed to more interests.

3. You learn more varied communication skills, such as how to deal with conflict and how to confront in a tactful way.

4. The cost of living is less because you have more people with whom to split the rent.

Cons of Living with Several Roommates

1. Usually there is more conflict. More people, more distinct personalities, different perspectives, and varied ways of doing things have the potential for greater misunderstanding and conflict.

2. It will be more difficult to get time alone.

3. Sometimes it will be more difficult to accomplish tasks that you want to accomplish simply because of the constant activity, sheer number of people, and potential distractions.

4. More roommates produce a more stressful environment, with a hustle of activity, phone ringing, and people visiting.

5. You may get lost in the shuffle. Your roommates won't always be able to socialize with you. So be sure to build friendships outside your household.

6. One more word of caution: with multiple roommates, you'll need to be more flexible and tolerant.

Pros of Living with One Other Person

1. You will have more time to yourself.

2. The pace will often be slower.

3. The potential for conflict is less because you have fewer people with whom to interact.

4. You have a greater opportunity to get to know one person well.

Cons of Living with One Other Person

1. Your roommate may not be around much or may be dating, and then you have very little opportunity to spend time with someone.

2. If you have a tense situation, you have no one else living there to help mediate.

After you know the answer to "How many roommates?" ask the question: "What kind?" What kind of roommate(s) do you prefer? Roommates who are your best friends? Roommates with whom you can spend a lot of your free time and talk often? Someone who will motivate you to do certain things, like exercise, go out, read good books? Or do you want to go for more independence? In other words, do you want a roommate who will split the bills with you, but who will leave you alone so you can come and go as you wish?

Or do you want a more committed person with whom to share your life?

There is another issue that is helpful to discuss in determining a roommate. That is living style. Do you spend a lot of time at home? Or do you simply want a place for eating and sleeping? Will you be relatively alone at work and want to come home to some people and activity, or are you dealing with people all day and want to be alone and quiet when you arrive home?

When you've thought about those issues, it's time to look for one or a few people to become your roommate(s). Let friends know, post a notice at your church, look around. Be specific when meeting potential roommates. Share your tastes and get to know theirs. Be specific about how you answered the questions above and specific, too, about values and irritations. Discuss the boyfriends/girlfriends issue so you don't end up with a "third roommate." Be specific about expectations, time together, and volume of music. And once you're committed to rooming together, take time to communicate regularly with each other and schedule some time for a weekly dinner or other activities together. The person with whom you room might become one of those cherished lifelong friends.

Loneliness

Once in awhile, no matter what you do, the relational aspect of life doesn't come together like you'd wish. Loneliness may become an issue for the very first time in your life. How do you deal with that new experience? How does loneliness become a temporary asset instead of a long-term liability?

Let's go back to Kelly Lunda, who experienced loneliness in her move to Washington. Here's what

Kelly says: "I prepared myself and assumed I would be lonely. It wasn't a 'resigned loneliness' but a more 'purposeful loneliness.' I was setting myself up, knowing I would be forced to turn to God and my faith. I also knew that this time would force me to be more self-reliant, to take initiative in areas I otherwise would have depended on my dad, brother, or friends to handle. So, although I knew the feelings of loneliness would be painful at times, I also knew that this time of aloneness could be beneficial.

"I reminded myself that loneliness is part of life. I would often tell myself when I was lonely that it wasn't the *place* that caused my loneliness or the *fact* I had moved away. I knew there would have been times of loneliness even if I had never moved 3,000 miles. Lonely times are part of life.

"I also reminded myself that you get lonely whether you're married or single. This is important for singles to remember. You can be surrounded by friends or have a spouse and still feel lonely.

"And finally, I reminded myself in the midst of the lonely times that the loneliness would pass. I tried not to dwell on it. I also tried to make sure I didn't feel sorry for myself, didn't isolate myself. I attempted to stay active and reach out to someone."

One final word from me. Don't let the pain of failed relationships, or relationships that didn't get off the ground, or relationships that changed or moved away keep you from pursuing people. Friendships are silver and gold, and they are worthy of pursuit.

CHAPTER 6

The Urge to Merge: Courtship and Engagement

One of the chief drives of the twentysomething person is to achieve intimacy. We long to develop a relationship with a close friend with whom we can share deeply.

In our twenties, some of us will move toward intimacy with that special person of the opposite sex. We will date. We will "fall" in love. We will consider marriage. We will get engaged. We will plan our wedding. We will marry.

Commenting on this phase of life, Doug Early says, "Once the degree has been pocketed, the next thing people expect is for you to find *someone*. But I say: Relax! If you should find someone, great. If you don't, *don't* force it. I think it's especially difficult on single Christians. Singles are often looked on as simply 'not married *yet*.' I find this truly sad. Not only does it make it difficult for those that are actually guided by the Lord to a single life, but it puts pressure on those who aren't to 'hurry up with it already.'"

Jim Francese has his own thoughts on the subject: "I think dating just to find a mate can be dangerous. As a single person, I felt a lot of pressure (some of it self-induced, to be sure) to find 'the one.' I nearly made disastrous decisions. Actually, I probably would have made them, but God prevented me from doing so. I think people in their twenties need to date to have fun and to get to know people. But don't date to find 'the one'; she or he will be discovered in due time."

Both Doug and Jim have pointed out some dangers in dating. However, don't give up dating just because it has some dangers. I think dating is important. For some reason, many Christian guys are either afraid to date or reluctant to do so. I've thought about it a great deal, and I've never figured out why. But the common refrain from many young women I know is that "Christian guys don't date." So, as I say to my college guys, "Gentlemen, start your engines." Date.

Starting Your Engines

Dating has advantages. Dating helps you develop your social skills. The dating process gives you confidence with members of the opposite sex. It lets you get to know more people. Dating teaches courtesy as you plan for another's benefit. Dating enhances conversational skills, widens horizons in knowing others, and broadens your range of exposure to new experiences like movies, plays, athletic events, hiking, and the like.

So, who should you date?

Probably the most natural way to date is to ask out people with whom you've already developed a relationship, like coworkers or people in your church.

Doug Early says this about pursuing relationships:

"This is an area in which I feel people should listen to their hearts, then act. In all relationships—with the opposite sex, the same sex, and even family members—when an opportunity arises to further a relationship—*take it!* All too often we let ourselves wonder what *might* happen if we do seize the opportunity. And all too often this wondering causes fear and paralysis.

"I have experienced very few people in this world who don't appreciate authentic action—those actions coming straight from your heart. And I can speak from experience. I have been crushed deeply and loved dearly, but I have never felt ashamed of speaking or acting honestly from the heart. I know, in the long run, and sometimes the run is long indeed, that risking in matters of the heart is the better option than not. I don't have as much going for me as a lot of guys I'm friends with, but I've dated and been friends with some truly amazing girls because I was willing to put my soul into the friendship. And that's where truly special relationships originate and dwell—in the soul."

As you date and get to know others, don't try to fill a void in your life that only God can fill by looking for that ultimate fulfillment in another person. Pascal said there is a God-shaped vacuum in the hearts of all of us that can be filled by Christ alone. Don't look for a mere human being to fill that place.

God desires that we have healthy relationships. But God knows that only he can meet our deepest needs. The Bible promises that God's Spirit alone can produce what we need. It is the Holy Spirit that produces in us "love, joy, peace, patience, kindness, goodness, faithfulness, gentleness and self-control" (Galatians 5:22). We need a healthy relationship both with God and with others to be truly fulfilled. It is important to discover which needs God alone can meet and which needs people can meet. Many times we expect people to do for us what God alone can do, and we expect God to do alone what people need to do in a relationship with us. And part of that relational aspect of our lives involves dating.

The Dating Process: Time, Commitment, Communication

Dating is not static. Instead, it is progressive. You can't date forever. As the relationship grows and develops, different dynamics come into play.

For a relationship to grow in a healthy way there needs to be balance. One key factor in the balance equation is *time*. The amount of time you spend with a person is very influential in the development of a relationship. There is no substitute for hours logged over weeks and months to naturally reveal a person and bond you to someone. Long, intense conversations over a few days will not substitute for the slow ripening and proving effect of time.

Another factor is *commitment*. The commitment level of a relationship must be honest and verifiable. Making a rash commitment will not cement an unstable relationship; however, an appropriate commitment gives a relationship structure and security.

The third factor in this equation is *communication*. There is a tendency in casual dating to go "too deep too fast." This applies to both verbal communication and to sexual activity. An honest, intimate form of communication is a goal to be desired in courtship, but if the intensity of communication becomes too deep it can actually erode instead of build a relationship that is too new to have such information shared. The opposite is also true: to share verbally on a trivial level when the relationship has lasted many months and there is a declaration of growing commitment is also hurtful.

The rule of thumb for these three factors is to keep them in balance. Perhaps these four diagrams will help.

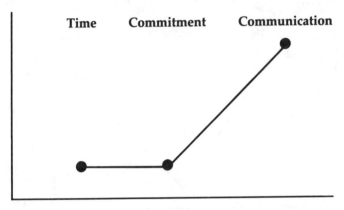

Figure 1

In figure 1, the dating relationship is fairly new. There is no solid commitment, yet the communication level has become intense either verbally or sexually or both. This level of communication has become a destabilizing force in the relationship.

In figure 2, the situation is different. This couple has dated for over a year. Their friendship has grown; their communication has deepened. Yet the tension grows because of the pressure to make a commitment. This couple should probably look at formally establishing more permanence in their relationship or think about breaking up. Convenience or familiarity or the fear of loneliness or of breaking up are not good enough reasons to avoid facing honestly and openly the next step in what has been a very good relationship. It's good to remember that only one dating relationship

45

ends in marriage. *All* others have to end somehow. The skill in dating is to know how and when to stop dating. Hopefully, the process will leave the other person better and more enriched after the initial disappointment of the break-up.

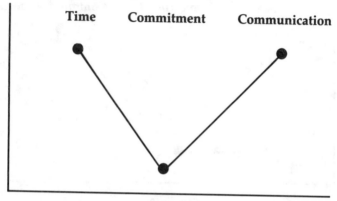

Figure 2

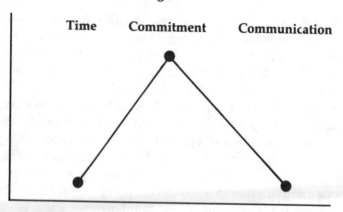

Figure 3

In figure 3, this couple has also created some instability, but through a rash commitment that can not be supported by either time or through a deepening level of communication. If the communication level does not become more intimate and the time increased, most likely the commitment will not be maintained.

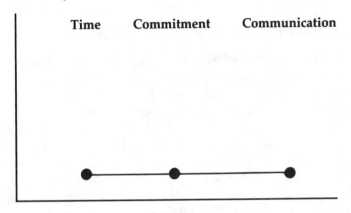

Time   Commitment   Communication

Figure 4

Figure 4 portrays the ideal relationship. It shows a good balance between time, commitment, and communication.

Balance is the key. It is fine to be casual in your communication in a new relationship. Too intense, too fast could topple the relationship when the roots of time and commitment are not there. On the other hand, if you've spent lots of time with someone, realize that at some point you will need to decide either to move forward or break up. Don't monopolize someone's dating time just to have someone to date. And don't rush the decision making prematurely. But keep in mind the balance between time, commitment, and communication.

Men and women have different struggles when it comes to balance. It seems that men lean toward "involvement" and are slow to make a "commitment." Women have to watch that they don't push the commitment prematurely. Women need to allow themselves to get to know the person before going for the "commitment contract."

On Making the Most of Relationships

Once the newness wears off, how do you continue to make a relationship sparkle? And, as familiarity and intimacy increase, how do you handle your sexual desires in a responsible manner?

One key concept in any relationship—dating, courtship, or marriage—is not to take your friend or friendship for granted. Dan Ibabao asks, "How often do we take for granted the one who loves us? Stop, look, appreciate the one who loves you despite all the little quirks. Realize that relationships can and do work. Some couples make it look easy, but everyone should know: 'If all the work is done by one, it won't be very much fun.'"

As you begin to think about marriage and engagement, don't be afraid to tackle the hard questions. Confront the issues of life: money, morals, values, where to live, family, careers, and more.

And listen carefully to what your loved one is saying. Far too often when we talk, we're so excited to contribute our thoughts, we jump in, running over the thoughts and comments of our companion. Or we naturally assume we know the answer to a question we've asked.

Now That We're Engaged

What happens once we decide to get engaged? Jim and Lisa Francese share one warning, "Sexual purity during engagement is very important. God clearly states that sex is for marriage only. Premarital sex can cause guilt that affects and disturbs the sex relationship after marriage. Lisa and I set a curfew so we wouldn't end up at someone's house, late, alone. We also had strict rules about what was allowed sexually during our engagement and what wasn't. Some people may not need all these constraints. We did. Also, praying together when we were feeling weak helped. God wants us to be obedient. If we let him, he will give us the power to do it. Lisa and I were able to abstain from sexual intercourse during our engagement and dating. We are so glad we did. To wait is difficult but definitely worth it."

Sue Harris, who married Stu two years ago, also has some ideas on engagement. "Work on communication, on being able to share with one another. Stu and I were in a small group together. That got us in the habit of sharing spiritually and praying together. I recommend a small group with some other couples. The second thing I recommend for a couple is some kind of premarital counseling. In addition to the counseling we received from the pastors who married us, we also profited from Engagement Encounter. Engagement Encounter opened us up to some big topics, which came in handy later because we already knew our mate's feelings and positions on some difficult subjects. Finally, I'd suggest that a couple find an older couple to help walk them through the engagement and early stages of marriage. We had two couples who were especially helpful to us."

Dating, courtship, engagement. These three steps lead us to marriage, the subject of chapter 7.

CHAPTER 7

And Suddenly, You're Married

There you are. One moment, you're single. The next, married. You're standing in front of the church waiting for your bride to walk down the aisle. Or, you're the bride, clinging tightly to Dad's arm, looking down that long aisle at the guy to whom you'll soon be pledging your commitment for life.

Sure, you haven't felt completely single and unattached during your courtship and engagement. But in just a matter of moments, any remote possibilities of remaining single will suddenly vanish. Yet you look forward to that moment. You love that person in front of you. You desire a relationship of honesty, intimacy, and accountability. You've thought about this decision carefully and you're ready to take the step.

The wedding ceremony begins. The music, the message, the Scripture, the rings, the vows. You hear yourself "pledging your troth," and then suddenly you're married.

Married and in your twenties—an interesting place to be. Let's discuss that place and the relationship you have with your new lifetime partner, your spouse. To help me with that task I've asked married couples in their twenties or early thirties to share with you what they have been learning about marriage.

I chose six couples: Jim and Lisa Francese, who have been married two years and have no children; Stu and Sue Harris, who have been married two years and now teach English in Japan and have no children; Bob and Tracy Regan, who have been married for seven years and have two young children; Eric and Lisa Kragerud, who have been married three years and have no children; Tim and Carroll Snow, who are just entering their thirties, have two children, and have been married eleven years; Steve and Lisa Call, who have been married four years and have one newborn; and Mark and Virginia Larson, also in their thirties, married ten years, and also the parents of two children. (You will, by the way, hear from the Snows, the Regans, the Calls, the Larsons, and others when we discuss having children in the next chapter.) My wife and I added some of our thoughts as well.

But before we dive into some principles for successfully maintaining a strong marriage, let's look at some of these couples and how they approached marriage.

Mark and Virginia Larson married right out of college. The benefits they see in that decision are that they were not yet set in their ways, they could discover what life was like together, and they didn't carry a lot of "bachelor baggage" with them. But they had an interesting dynamic going. Virginia was the *last* of her friends to be married. Mark was the *first* of his friends to be married. So Mark was ignorant about weddings (and married life, for that matter) and Virginia was very knowledgeable on both subjects from spending so much time talking to her friends.

As they moved into marriage, Virginia's greatest concern was deciding what their own marriage would look like and how she and Mark would develop their goals together. She did not want to emulate her parents' marriage and was anxious to establish a solid relationship and home. Virginia and Mark wanted their marriage to be different from the norm of society. They believed that Christ could make their marriage abundantly alive in the midst of a dying society. And they spent a lot of time talking about this important subject.

But in the midst of serious discussions, they also had a lot of fun. Here's how Mark describes what happened. "We had no real preconceived ideas of what life was like, so we allowed ourselves to have fun. We were deeply in love when we got married and we still are. But we owe our success in marriage not to the fact that we are 'right' for each other but to the fact that Christ has brought us together and wants our marriage to succeed."

Bob and Tracy Regan went into their marriage with stereotypes of what they wanted their spouse to be. Bob was looking for "June Cleaver" (of *Leave It to Beaver* fame), the perfect wife and homemaker. Tracy was looking for a "sexy Mr. Rogers." Neither, obviously, found their stereotype in their mate.

What they found was a big challenge early in marriage. Tracy became pregnant six months after they were married. Within fifteen months (for the non-math majors reading this book, that's six months plus nine months of pregnancy), they went from being single to being a family before they had had a chance to build a solid marriage. They discovered quickly the difficulty of maintaining a good marriage with kids. It was even tougher on Bob than it was on Tracy. He had to adjust to graduation, marriage, children, and a new job within a short period of time—all with new demands and expectations.

In the midst of the difficulties, they discovered that the greatest joy in their marriage was their friendship!

They really liked each other as friends. They also met their difficulties with two principles they held tightly. First, they believed that with faith in God, all things were possible. And second, they believed that if they worked at it, God would show them the good in each other and change whatever unrealistic expectations they might have had.

Steve and Lisa Call were married right out of college (they wanted to get married while in college but were glad they waited). They were young and felt, like the Larsons, that their youth was a plus because they weren't set in their ways and could discover how to live life together without a lot of preconceived notions or excess baggage.

Steve's big fears going into marriage were that he'd never be able to play hoops (he's a basketball junkie) with the guys anymore and that he would lose his individuality. But he discovered that wasn't true at all. He discovered that he and Lisa didn't spend every minute together, and they both felt good about continuing their relationships with friends from college. Steve also went into the marriage with few expectations, and consequently, he feels marriage is "ten times better than I expected."

Lisa, on the other hand, had higher expectations and found marriage a bit tougher. She had to learn how to be accountable to one other person, and the "learning as you go" aspect of marriage was a bit harder for her.

Although their marriage has been relatively easy in terms of adjustments, they have experienced a couple of areas of struggle. Dealing with other relationships has been one area: how do you keep in touch and relate to parents, close friends, and acquaintances and still keep the marriage a top priority? They also have had to work at getting to know their spouse's friends when some of those people might not be the kind of people with whom they'd normally spend time.

The Larsons. The Regans. The Calls. Three couples who began married life early in their twenties. Using their experience and the insights of others, let's look at a few principles that will help you if you marry in your twenties.

1. *Enjoy whatever time alone you may have.* There are some tremendous advantages to being married in your twenties. One is that you'll probably be able to spend some quality and quantity time together before children join you. I do premarital counseling. Those who get married in their thirties and who want children tend to have them more quickly than those who marry in their twenties. The biological clocks of those in their thirties are running down and they, out of necessity, want children more quickly. But in the twenties, you have more time. You are alone—just the two of you—with very few other family demands. Enjoy this time to the full. Never again will you be in this situation.

I love children. I have four of them. I like the kids in the neighborhood and the children in the church. I enjoy watching them, listening to them, having them around. But once you have children, they will either be physically in your home or literally occupying your mind while they are away. One of my convictions in life is "you never stop being a parent." Even when your kids grow up and move out, you still think, care, and pray about them. You are never released from being a parent. And if you should be so unfortunate as to lose a child to death, memories of that child occupy your mind much as if that child still lived on earth. But for now, in the early stages of marriage, it's just the two of you. That can be a blessing: it's just the two of us!

And it can be a struggle: oh no, it's just the two of us! See it as a blessing and not as a curse.

2. *Shift your focus.* Stu Harris says, "Marriage involves a complete shifting of focus from what *I* want, to what's good for *us*. What makes it difficult is that 'what I want' does not just go away. It comes back again and again. It may show itself in the smallest of things. I imagine it's a lifetime struggle.

"I am also struck by how clearly our own weaknesses show themselves when we try to truly love another person. Nothing short of God's grace and love make a marriage work. The mystery lies somewhere in allowing God to love us so completely, that we are able to freely and selflessly love our mates. This too seems to be a lifelong journey."

3. *Remember whom you married (and for how long).* Elisabeth Elliot, in a speech to newly engaged couples, said these true and lasting words: "When you marry, you both think you are getting a prize package, but what you are really getting is a surprise package!"

Lisa Kragerud says, "Realize when you marry someone you are not inheriting royalty—Prince or Princess Charming—you are inheriting a family member. Now think what it was like with your family. When you were growing up, your brothers or sisters got completely on your nerves. They borrowed your clothes, they switched the TV channel when you were watching it, and so on. You could have a pretty nasty fight with them, and then you went to school and would forget all about it. During recess you saw a kid picking on them and you rushed to their defense. No matter what fight you had had previously, they were your siblings and you loved them forever.

"You have to take the same attitude with the person you marry. It is natural to argue and when you do, the worst thing to say is, 'How could we fight like that and think we were right for each other? Maybe this marriage was a mistake!' Did you expect, growing up, that you would never fight with your family?

"When you did disagree, did you say you were sorry, or did you say, 'Let's agree to never fight again?'

"The last thing you should think when you've had a spat with your spouse is that if only you can get through this, you will be so in love, and you will never go through it again. The key to love is commitment, not 'never fighting again,' and if you can think of your spouse as a forever family member, it will not panic you when you fight.

"If you can stop panicking every time you disagree, eventually it will lead to fewer fights. Or at least, you won't remember them, because you now see disagreeing not as a statement of your marriage, but as an inevitable consequence of living with someone day in and day out."

Okay, so you didn't marry Prince or Princess Charming. Another thing to remember is that the person you did marry will not be the same person later in life. Bob and Tracy Regan say this, "What you see is not what you get. That person you walk down the aisle with on your wedding day is *not* the same person you will be married to five or ten years from now! People change— we are supposed to. Change is the result of growing and expanding in our understanding of God, ourselves, and our world. Successful marriages are the ones that continually rediscover themselves."

Almost everyone I know who is married has a time or two early in the marriage process when they ask the question, "Did I really marry the right person? I can't believe the person I married would act like this. Was it God's will for me to marry him/her?" My answer to these questions is this: these are not the questions to ask *after* you're married. They are questions to be asked *before* marriage. The point is: you're married, so get on with it. Bob and Tracy say, "We believe that God can multiply the blessings of a marriage in the same way that Jesus multiplied the five loaves and two fish to feed a multitude. Let him take what you have and multiply it and bless you in the process."

4. *Learn how to resolve conflict.* Lisa Francese says, "Obviously many adjustments need to be made in a new marriage. One of the major areas for Jim and me in our first year was learning how to resolve conflict. We came from different family backgrounds and have different personalities. He likes to 'stew' for a while, think, calm down, pray, and *then* talk. I'm ready to start talking and forgiving in about two minutes. He needs more like fifteen or twenty. The difference of thirteen to eighteen minutes has been a nightmare if I don't back off and let him gain perspective. I still struggle with this issue because my needs for love, acceptance, and forgiveness sometimes overshadow my concern for his needs of time, space, and quietness. We have both made this a matter of prayer and God has been faithful in helping us consider the needs of our spouse."

The Krageruds have this to say about conflict: "Most newly married couples are extremely idealistic. They feel that to have the perfect marriage they should rarely argue, and when they do, the communication should be something out of one of the books they've read—where you speak calmly, give the other person his turn at perfect intervals, make sure each partner has been heard. What a shock when the first little 'spat' is an exchange of loud voices talking over one another and someone leaves the room in a huff!

"Because the expectation level of newly married

couples can be so high, really petty disagreements and irritations may seem like huge crises where each person has to apologize repeatedly and the husband has to send roses. Of course he only said that the meat loaf tasted a little funny, but when you are self-examining your marriage to death, this may seem like a major issue!"

In resolving conflict, an important consideration is to get the issue(s) out in the open before it's too late.

Lisa Kragerud warns, "There are times when your spouse will just get on your nerves. Maybe he or she is chronically late, leaves the milk out, forgets to lock the door, and squeezes the toothpaste from the wrong end. This is normal and inevitable. How do you know when the quibbling is not normal, not inevitable, and has even gotten dangerous? Many couples in the process of divorce will admit that the problem started many years before divorce was even mentioned. Maybe at the beginning of their marriage, the husband repeatedly made decisions without asking his wife, and she, wanting to be the 'good wife,' pretended it did not bother her at all. Deep inside, however, she was harboring bitterness against her husband about it. Fifteen years later she walks out on him and he cannot figure out what he did wrong.

"Maybe the wife criticizes the husband constantly and after awhile, he feels like whatever he says or does is wrong. So instead of trying to improve, he buries himself in his work, television, newspaper, hobbies, *anything* to drown out the nagging. Seven years later the wife files for divorce, complaining that her husband never communicates with her and now they don't even know each other anymore! How different these two scenarios would be if the wife had told her husband she wanted to help in the decision making and if the husband had told the wife she was killing his self-esteem!"

Taking the advice of the Franceses and the Krageruds, we find that the first steps in conflict resolution are

● Don't be unrealistic about conflicts; they will happen in every marriage.

● Bring the conflict out into the open.

● Be sensitive to how your spouse works on resolution and compromise your style somewhat so that both of you can be part of the solution.

● Pray about the conflict and ask God for his wisdom and guidance in the matter.

But what happens if openness and sensitivity don't work? What then? How do you know when you should go for help?

Lisa and Eric offer their thoughts on this matter. "Most unhealthy marriage patterns begin the first year of marriage, and yet, how many people actually go for help their first year of marriage? If more would, less would experience *real* problems later.

"We suggest that you select a counselor when you're in the midst of engagement and planning the wedding. Carefully select the pastor who officiates at your wedding. Choose a pastor who is there to counsel you in your engagement, who wants more than anything for your marriage to work out, and who, through the process of premarital counseling, gets to know you and your spouse. This is one reason why it is so important for you and your spouse to be committed to a church. The same person who marries you will be the person who you can first go to when you hit that dead-end road in communication. If you have a person to talk to with whom you and your spouse feel comfortable, it will be that much easier to go to that person when you need him or her.

"Why don't people go for help more? First, they don't know when they really need help, and second, they're too prideful. Most people are concerned about how it will look to other people when they hear you've only been married three months and you already need help. 'Besides,' they think, 'our problem will work itself out; we don't need help until it gets serious.' How ridiculous!

"If you were a new mother and your infant were crying all the time, would you just hope that it would go away? Or would you call someone for help? If you're a new mother, you can't expect to know exactly what to do. The same thing is true in marriage. As a new husband or wife, you can't expect to know what to do. We suggest the first time you and your spouse are stumped about a problem such as leadership, sex, finances, in-laws, or any of the other things on the top ten list of things to argue about, you call your pastor immediately. Do not—we repeat—*do not* let things fester, even for a day, or you will start to develop patterns that can last a lifetime."

Lisa and Eric continue, "Does that mean that every time you have a fight you should run for help? No, let's not get extreme. You need to go for help when you have a problem that doesn't end with a solution you can agree upon."

The Krageruds throw in one more analogy: "Just remember, if your faucet continued to leak and you couldn't seem to fix it yourself no matter how many home fix-it books you read, you would probably call a professional. Isn't your marriage worth as much to you—and more—as your faucet?"

I had the privilege of being the pastor who married

Lisa and Eric. They have a strong marriage but it is not without its conflicts. They have been conscientious about resolving conflicts, and I'm very proud of them. Their advice can be well taken.

5. *Beware of time and money.* Dr. James Dobson says that fatigue and time pressure are two of the greatest hindrances to marriage. I agree. We get on the fast track and have trouble scheduling time for our spouse. And when we do get together, we are often drained and fatigued from the pace we've endured.

My wife and I try to counteract that pressure by regularly scheduling date nights or date afternoons. We try (and I emphasize *try*) to book those dates when we are at our best, not worst. We also try to get the occasional weekend getaway. And we work at keeping a Sabbath—one day during the week when we concentrate on our marriage and family and don't get run ragged doing errands, working on projects, and attending meetings.

Now a word about money. Tim Snow graduated from Fuller Theological Seminary with an emphasis in Marriage and Family. He says, "I think money is the number-one problem area in a marriage because it expresses so much. It provides a battleground in marriage."

Tim's right. In our culture, money symbolizes success. Money symbolizes worth—if they don't pay you what you think they should, it seems to be a statement about how much they really value you. To in-laws and family members, money signifies how well you're taking care of your spouse. How you spend your money will indicate where your priorities are. And the spending of money is where the battle lines are often drawn in marriage. How will we spend what we have? Whose priority has top priority? Is the next major purchase a VCR or some drapes? How can we get more money to buy this "thing" that seems so necessary? What are our family's priorities and how can we reflect those priorities in the way we spend our money? The making of money can also complicate our understanding of the roles of husband and wife. Tim says that was difficult for him when he was in seminary and his wife was the chief breadwinner.

The secret to the money issue is communication. Talk about what you're earning, what you're spending, and how you're feeling about the money issues. Communicate about a budget and what you'll do with any discretionary income.

But no matter how much communication is done, money may still be a headache in your marriage. The key is not to let it become a cancer that destroys.

6. *Plan some ways you can learn and grow in your marriage.* Do you want your marriage to be fruitful and rewarding? Then use some of the tools and strategies mentioned below, which will help you grow in your marriage.

Most of the couples contributing to this chapter agreed on one piece of advice: the importance of being in contact with other young couples, preferably a group of young couples "where you can have open and frank discussions regarding your marriage."

Others stressed heavily the need to have relationships with older couples where you are free to ask the "what next" questions. What's the next stage in marriage going to be like (first child, second child, teenagers) and how can we best prepare for that? What are the goods and bads in marriage? The necessary and unnecessary? The point is: how can we learn from others who have already walked the part of the marriage road that we're now on? Having a few older married adults as friends is a good way to prepare for the future and process the present.

Another way is to attend marriage and family seminars in your area. Marriage Encounter is one. Church marriage and family weekends are great resources as well. And if you think you can't afford it (the money issue again), realize that the money invested in your marriage may be the best investment you could ever make.

Another good way to learn is to read a book together as a couple. Lisa Francese says, "A book that has been very helpful to our marriage is *Marriage Takes More Than Love* by Jack and Carol Mayhall. The book concerns the choices we make in marriage. We choose to love and be loved or to turn inward. We choose to accept or reject our spouse. We choose to forgive, communicate, understand, admire, and grow. We also choose or reject God's lordship in our marriage. This book has been a blessing to us. We read it aloud, discuss one main point each, and then pray. The act of reading a book together and talking and praying together is a special activity that has helped us grow closer."

Other couples have recommended *The Marriage Builder* by Larry Crabb, *The Language of Love* by Gary Smalley and John Trent, and *As for Me and My House* by Walter Wangerin, Jr. The number of books on marriage seems endless. Good authors include James Dobson, Norm Wright, Ed and Gloria Wheat, Charlie Shedd, and others. You don't have to read them all. But just the process of sitting down together and reading and talking about the goals of your marriage is a very helpful endeavor.

7. *Work hard at and be creative in your marriage.* Stu Harris says, "The first years of marriage can set habits

for life. Work hard on your marriage and get help from other couples."

Tim and Carroll Snow say, "You need to constantly look for new ways to affirm your spouse. Get out of your relational ruts. And even if you don't feel like it all the time, continue to show love for, a desire in, and a belief in the other person."

To do what Stu and the Snows are saying takes work and commitment. In marriage, you can easily irritate your spouse. When that happens neither person feels creative or anxious to show love, express affection, or affirm each other, but you do it anyhow because you're committed. And that takes work and effort.

8. *Decide on some "non-negotiables."* In other words, decide on some rules in your marriage that are not open to debate. Choose some guidelines, some rules, some patterns for living that you will follow.

Here are Tim and Carroll Snow's rules, which they developed as a reaction to their own families of origin.

● *Affirmation and affection.* We will affirm and be affectionate with one another. In the course of struggles, we will not withhold affirmation or affection from each other.

● *Expression of anger and frustration.* We will attempt to be honest with each other and to receive what the other is saying. We will strive not to be people who are "bottled up" but, instead, people who can express what is on their minds.

● *Money.* We will talk about money, be open about it. We know this subject has the potential for great misunderstanding in our marriage. We will monitor this subject closely and talk about feelings, priorities, and spending patterns.

Here are Mark and Virginia Larson's.

● *Friendship.* We are to be each other's companion,

confidant, and friend. This friendship factor is as important as the sexual relationship we have in marriage.

● *Commitment.* We accept that this friendship will be difficult to maintain, but we are committed to investing time, energy, and hard work in it.

Let me close with a few final comments from our contributing couples.

"Marriage is great because it allows you to treat someone in a way that confirms his or her great worth and incredible value. As humans, it is easy for us to accept the fact that others may be accepted despite their faults, but when it comes to our own life, it's a different story. Therefore, a marriage lets you see you are loved through your faults and illustrates God's love for us." (Tim and Carroll Snow)

"The biggest joy for both of us is knowing that no matter what you do or say, you are still loved." (Steve and Lisa Call)

"Two gifts that have enhanced our marriage are the ability to communicate and the great desire to forgive one another." (Bob and Tracy Regan)

This closes our thoughts on marriage. Now let's see how children impact our lives in our twenties.

CHAPTER 8

Here Come the Kids

I was twenty-nine when Heather arrived at our home. Life has never been the same since. After Heather came Josh, then Jeremy, and finally Jon. As I write this chapter they are fifteen (almost sixteen and driving!), fourteen, eight, and five. When Heather turned thirteen, I realized I would be a parent of a teenager for the next seventeen years!

My life has been impacted by kids. My life revolves around family. It's the dominating story in my life, even more so than my job. And it all began when I was twentysomething.

What's it like to have kids? In the words of my friends, Tim and Carroll Snow, "You'll never know until they arrive!" And they are right. Despite all the preparation for childbirth and child rearing you might make, you're still surprised when the child actually arrives.

But the surprise can be modified from "totally surprised" to "somewhat surprised," and that's why we're devoting a chapter to kids even though having children may be one of the furthest subjects from your mind at this time. To help you understand what happens when children enter your life in your twenties (and beyond, for that matter), I wanted to write this chapter. And, as I've done with most chapters, a bunch of my friends helped, friends who have children that range in age from five years to ten weeks old.

Marriage and Children

One purpose God had in mind when he created marriage was that of reproduction. The human race would continue as couples gave birth to and then trained their children.

Some couples dream of having children. They can hardly wait to fill the rooms of their homes with offspring. They may have come from happy families where the mother loved being a mom and the father loved being a dad. They want children that take after them, and they're anxious to have the first child arrive.

Other couples are in the postponement mode. They postpone a family in order to give more time to "just the two of us." Or they delay having kids until they finish school or to allow them to pursue twin careers.

Pros and Cons of Having Kids in Your Twenties

So what's the wisest thing to do? Have kids in your twenties? Or wait until you're more mature? Let's look at the pros and the cons of having children in your twenties.

There are some tremendous advantages to beginning your family in your twenties. You get to grow up with your kids, for one. You also have more energy and the resources of youth. And you are usually more flexible than you are in your thirties.

If you wait until your thirties to have a child, you might not be as fertile. My wife expresses another downside of waiting: "You have more wisdom, but less energy with which to impart it." And when you're forty and you still have toddlers (the result of beginning parenthood in your thirties and having more than one child), you may wish you had begun earlier.

The plus side of waiting is that you do have more family security. You've been married longer. Your marriage is probably more stable. You've enjoyed a few extra years alone together. The wife may have had time to pursue a career and may not have that feeling of "unfinished business" or "what would have happened if I'd pursued a career and not had the kids so early."

So what happens when the kids come, regardless of whether you're twentysomething, thirtysomething, or even in your forties?

What Happens When You Bring Them Home: The Blessings

Let my friends and me tell you about some of the joys of being a parent.

1. *Kids can be a lot of fun.* We laugh a lot at our house. We also cry for the same reason—the kids. My kids make me laugh; they bring me joy through their actions and their words. As Art Linkletter said years ago, "Kids say the darndest things." They do. Their smiles, actions, and responses make you laugh. There would be a lot less sparkle in my life without my kids.

2. *Love takes on a whole new meaning.* You've learned a lot about love from your relationship with your spouse, but you learn much more through having children. Your love for your children is incredible. For the first time you will understand what love your mom and dad must have extended to you, and you will begin to grasp how great the love of God is for his children. The dimensions and dynamics of love explode when your child comes home.

3. *You learn to practice new virtues.* You may have talked about virtues like serving, compromise, and forgiveness, but when you have children you learn to *live* those virtues.

4. *You experience "family joy" and "family identity."* You discover the simple joys of shared time together, silly games, and both quiet and noisy moments. You discover that bedtime is sacred, that those times of tucking your child in, reading a story, and saying goodnight prayers are truly special. You discover that a family is more than a group of individuals—it is a corporate entity with its own personality and identity.

5. *You enjoy God's blessings on your family.* As you have children, you understand the blessing of obeying the commandment to be fruitful and multiply. You see how the fulfillment of that desire not only keeps the human race going but also blesses you in many ways.

What Happens When You Bring Them Home: The Challenges

But having kids doesn't touch only the plus side of life. Raising children also presents new challenges from the minute you bring your baby boy or girl home from the hospital.

1. *You experience total responsibility from which you can never escape.* This feeling of total responsibility impacted Tim and Carroll Snow. The fact that they couldn't run from this situation seemed almost overwhelming, as it does with almost every parent I know.

2. *You are forced to rearrange your schedule.* Scheduling around three people is difficult, especially when one of the three is totally dependent and needs constant care.

You must readjust your expectations of your "free time" and "your needs." Tim said that he found himself giving up his "previous needs" like regular exercise. With the coming of the kids, there just wasn't the time or the opportunity for exercise.

Not everyone will have to give up exercise when children come, but most new parents will find their schedules revamped and something missing from their schedule that formerly was a source of joy or pride. For me it was athletics. Since we had children, I've not been able to play as much racquetball, tennis, or basketball as I'd like. My reading has also been curtailed some. I know it's not that I'm a poor planner or time manager. I am fairly good at those organizational skills. It's just that when something is added to your life (and having a child is a big "something"), something must be taken away. You have to be ready for that when the baby arrives.

3. *Your marriage relationship is impacted.* Tim said this about his two kids and the effect it had on his marriage, "With each child, there was a period of resentment, but not toward them. Instead, I directed the resentment toward my wife, because she was demanding so much more of me. I had to realize that I was in a *co*-parenting role. The sad thing is that I didn't realize the source of this resentment cognitively. I couldn't explain it, but I could feel it!"

Because so much energy is expended on your kids, you will have less energy for your spouse. Fatigue will affect your communication. Because you need energy to love one another, you have to preserve some energy for your spouse and not expend it completely on other people, activities, and jobs.

4. *You need to adjust to life at home.* For the parent who stays home, there is a tremendous transition to make from full-time work and adult companionship to being around only a baby. Both Virginia Larson and Lisa Call stressed this. Lisa wants to be a full-time mother, but she decided she needed to work a few hours each week after the baby arrived to bring more adult interaction into her life. Virginia says that when you leave work the only "report card" you get is from your husband because you're not getting affirmation from your co-workers. That puts more pressure on the husband-wife relationship.

5. *You worry whether you're doing a good job.* Virginia Larson says, "Before my kids came, I wondered if I could really be a good mom. The amount of patience and commitment it took caused me to have great apprehensions ahead of time. And I still wonder if I'm doing all right."

What to Do Now that the Kid Is Home

Obviously this chapter is not going to be a manual on child rearing. There are many other fine books written on that subject. However, I would like to share a few principles for welcoming that chip off the old block into your home.

1. *Prepare yourself for having kids.* Hang out with families, talk with other couples, ask questions, read books on raising children. Even after you've done this, remember—you'll never be totally prepared for having children.

2. *Take inventory.* List the resources you have to give as a parent. And, remember, the greatest gifts you can give your children are time and the stability of your marriage.

3. *Be thankful.* Pray for your children with an attitude of thankfulness. Thank God for the nine months of

pregnancy he gives you so you can adjust to the fact that life will never be the same.

I'm glad I have kids. Of course, there are some times when I wish I could give them back. But I don't know where to return them and they probably wouldn't take them if I offered. I think their warranty has expired.

But on the whole, I'm glad Heather, Josh, Jeremy, and Jon have come to live at our house. And I'm glad God invented the idea of marriage and family, because having kids has greatly enriched my life. Life just isn't the same once you have kids—it's better.

CHAPTER 9

Being Single: The Good and the Difficult

All my friends are getting married
Still I go to hear them say,
"I will cherish you forever,
For today's our wedding day."
So I see them walk the aisle,
They walk right out of my life;
Being single has those times
That can cut just like a knife.

Being single is exciting,
At least that's what it's supposed to be;
Being married seems so stable,
It's a balance of extremes.
What I really want is both of these,
The fulfillment and the fun.
So for now I place my trust in You
That You'll complete what You've begun.

So give me single-minded love, Lord,
To make my life complete,
'Cause I don't want to worry anymore
About the one that I might meet.
Lord, I know You have a plan
Though at times it's hard to see,
So give me single-minded love
So I can give you all of me.

—Kenny Marks

A dilemma, isn't it? The single life is supposed to be exciting. I'm sure you've seen the bumper stickers, "Happiness is Being Single." But when we watch our friends get married, we long for what we see as the stability and companionship that comes through marriage.

We've looked at courtship, engagement, and marriage in previous chapters. But what if we're not in a serious relationship and it doesn't look like we're going to be in one for a while? What then?

Mike Neelley, a co-worker and single friend of mine, has these comments. "I was in seven weddings last summer, and my struggle was not in wanting to be married, but in the change in my relationships with my friends. I was no longer a priority for their free time. As the wedding approaches, they become more scarce.

"I've discovered that engagement is not merely a time for the engaged couple to prepare for a wedding and a life together; it is also a time for the unengaged to prepare for or learn what it means to have married friends. As an unengaged single, I must now pursue two people and arrange *three* schedules!

"But apart from weddings and the external pressure you may feel to be married, our time of singleness can be a positive time. Often we enter the 'pursuit mode' of relationships, feeling that if we only find the *right* person our lives will be better and more fulfilled. This can be true to an extent, but it can also be a dangerous fallacy. I believe in the statement, 'It is more important to *be* the right person than to *find* the right person.' It is a matter of giving versus taking. Approximately every four to six months, God goes out of his way to remind me of this.

"Singleness is a time when we are free from many ties, free to explore and discover who we are and what we want. If you are a people-pleaser like me, relationships often hold you back from this exploration because we have learned that often it is not safe to be ourselves. We cannot discover who we are if we're not being who we are because of a fear that someone may not like us.

"My roommate and I are having our mid-life crises at the age of twenty-six. Being single, we have great freedom to work through who we are, why we do what we do, and what we want. Being single is not a prerequisite for self-discovery, but it's been helpful for me."

Jim Francese was single for a few years in his twenties before getting married. Here's what he says about the solo experience: "A lot of single people (including me when I was single) tend to view singleness as an uncomfortable and somewhat unnatural state that we must get through before we meet Ms. Right or Mr. Right and get on with life. But singleness can be exciting, fun, and an excellent opportunity to 'get deep' with Jesus Christ. Once I started to let God really control my dating life, I saw how Jesus could meet my needs for friendship, companionship, and ways to fill my time. At times he did this through other people, and he also sent his Comforter, the Holy Spirit, to be with me.

"I have also been able to view the benefits of being single now that I'm a married man. Marriage is great and I'm thankful I'm married to Lisa, but your life does become more restricted and redirected when you are married, especially when children enter the picture. I will admit that the quality of my relationships with single people at work has deteriorated since I got married. I'm not saying this is inevitable, but it is harder to go to a movie with a single guy from work when Lisa is expecting me home in the evening.

"To single people I would say—live it up with Christ! Spend time with men and women friends. Go on missions. God can do unique things with single people."

Dan Ibabao is a single guy in his twenties who has followed Jim Francese's advice. Dan has won several Emmys as a sound engineer on television specials. As he's examined his life, he reflects, "There are things in this world we as single people can do more easily. We really have the ability to make time for others. If you are so inclined, volunteering with service organizations is a great outlet, and going on short-term missions is another opportunity to consider. Basically, the burdens and the responsibilities of a single person are much lighter, so go help the world around you. Touch and be touched."

Doug Early is a little more militant as he views the single lifestyle. "I think singleness is an issue that far too many Christians forget to consult God about. I have spent hours upon hours praying with the Lord about what is best for me. For a very long time, I always assumed I would marry. After much time with God, I'm no longer sure. I know in my heart one of the things that sets me apart right now is that I have no commitments and very few primary attachments. If the Lord guided me back to China again tomorrow [Doug spent a year teaching English there], I could go and not have to think first about what so-and-so feels. I am not ready to say one way or the other what the future holds, but at least I'm not presuming upon the Lord. I admit the pressure is great and sometimes the loneliness even more so, but dating and marriage are *not* for everyone."

Mike, Jim, Dan, and Doug have painted the picture. Singleness has its advantages, but the pressure is on to be married. And sometimes the pressure is so great that singleness seems like a curse instead of a blessing.

So how do we live life abundantly as single people in a world where couples predominate? I've asked some of my single friends (and some of my friends who were single in their twenties) to help you get a handle on singleness. Here's what they came up with.

The Benefits of Being Single

1. *Singleness gives great flexibility to life.* The twenties are a great time to go on adventures, to experiment with careers, to take a few risks, to travel, to do short-term missions. These adventures enhance a person's confidence, help provide a comprehensive worldview, and give a heightened sense of how much you can contribute. Doug Early served a year in China, as did my friend Peg Achterman. Jim Allen led a four-person team of folks in their twenties to serve Christ at the University of Jos in Nigeria. People who are committed to Christ, who have completed college, and who are unmarried can be like the elite paratroopers in an army. God can quickly shuttle you to wherever your skills are needed. That's excitement. That's adventure. That's flexibility.

2. *Friendships can be enhanced through singleness.* Jim Francese touched on this when he mentioned how he was more out of touch with his single buddies after he got married. And Mike lamented the fact that when his friends got married, they became more scarce. Unmarried people in their twenties tend to put constructive energy into relationships. They want to find and build friendships on a more intimate, stable, long-term basis. In the chapter on relationships, people in their twenties acknowledged how much more difficult it is to meet and spend time with people beyond college, but as a single person you will have more time and energy to pursue relationships. These friendships built in the twenties can be some of the most rewarding joys in life.

3. *Singleness allows you freedom in decision making and gives you the opportunity to take responsibility for the decisions made.* Growth comes from taking your own risks and either rising or falling by your decisions. When you are married, you learn different skills like compromise, teamwork, and deferring to others. But as a single person, you can use this time to learn one of the critical elements in personal maturity: taking responsibility for your own life. Married people also learn this trait, but they do so differently—they live as a team and concentrate more on interdependence than independence. I also believe that people who have learned how to take responsibility for their own lives before marriage make better marriage partners. They have learned to recognize their strengths and weaknesses, and they know what decision making takes. An immature adult usually blames others or puts too much responsibility on others close to them to meet their needs. Singleness allows you the time and opportunity to grow up. As Mike said, "It's more important to *be* the right person than to *find* the right person." Singleness allows time for both.

4. *Singleness gives you time to work on those rough or injured areas of your life.* The twenties are a time when you have a more developed sense of your own identity. However, due to the breakdown of family structure and nurture through divorce or other dysfunctions, adolescence is prolonged for some people into their twenties. I've seen this often in working with students. They need *time* to come to grips with what happened in childhood and to work at repairing their relationship

Being Single: The Good and the Difficult

with their parents. In some cases, individuals feel inadequate to marry because of missing or sketchy role models. Not all people are ready for intimacy or marriage in their twenties. Singleness allows you some time to work on these areas of hurt.

With these thoughts in mind, let's discuss ways we can maximize our single lives.

Maximum Living as a Single Person

Here are some positive steps to make these solo years count.

1. *Thank God that you're single.* Life is a gift! At every stage God enables you to live life to the fullest. God is sovereign (Psalm 139), he works all things together for good to those that love him (Romans 8:28), and he has some great ideas in mind for you now (Jeremiah 29:11).

Many single people I've met don't appreciate their singleness as a gift. And that's because they've always been single! They have taken their singleness for granted. See your singleness as a gift from God and give thanks.

If you've had trouble being thankful for being single, I'd like to suggest that you do a little exercise. First, make a list of what makes you unique. Then make a list of how God has blessed you. Then list the trials you're facing and the resources God has given you for meeting these trials. Then meditate on the truth of Jeremiah 29:11. Know that it was written for you. " 'For I know the plans I have for you,' declares the LORD, 'plans to prosper you and not to harm you, plans to give you hope and a future.' "

2. *Spend time with families.* Don't spend all your time hanging out with other singles. Almost everyone I talked to emphasized this. Doug Early made this comment, "For me it helps to be involved with families. Then I don't feel as if I'm missing out on so much."

Kelly Lunda adds, "I have found it helpful not to spend all my free time with other single people. You're all struggling with similar problems and can spend too much time talking about them. I also have kept in touch with young married couples and some families. It's great spending time with kids—it lightens you up and helps you forget yourself for a while. Plus you can provide free child care for couples who need a night out."

3. *Claim God's promises.* Remember: God knows your heart and needs. He'll never give you more than you can handle, but will give you the grace to live at every stage of your life. You may not always understand his plans and his timing, for his thoughts and ways are higher than yours, but he has great plans in mind for you.

Kelly comments, "God knows better than me *who* the best is for me. He also knows the best *time* better than me. I'd be compromising some of the abundant life he has for me if I hurried the process. If God has me single now, that's the best for me now. Any different would be second best."

4. *Give yourself time to build long-lasting relationships.* See your singleness as a gift to be able to do this.

5. *Work on the hurts and rough edges in your life.* Don't stuff time so full you can't think, and don't just push your problems aside. Take time to learn new patterns of relating other than the destructive ones you may have learned at home. Try to understand and forgive hurts from childhood, and look for more positive role models. As you find your true identity in Christ, ask God to help you grow into a healthy human being—a

person who can stand up straight and face the future, knowing that it is in God's hands.

6. *Be both reflective and relational.* Don't hide from yourself by constantly seeking out other people. Learn to enjoy the quiet moments of reflection and meditation. But don't become a recluse either; seek out relationships that challenge and support you. If you need help in this process, ask the advice of a pastor, a friend, or a counselor.

7. *Get yourself ready for whatever relationships God has in mind for you.* Begin to learn what unconditional love is all about. Dan Ibabao says, "I was involved in a relationship that lasted four years. Soon after the breakup, a friend came up to me and said, 'If you thought Jennifer was great, just wait for the next person the Lord has lined up for you!' Take care, be patient, and remember: relationships are like a garden. They take lots of nurturing and some weeding, but eventually they will blossom."

8. *Ask yourself two key questions:* What do I believe is my purpose in life? How can I *invest* my life, not just *spend* my time? Make the time count. Don't just see time as something you fill until you're married. Make it count now.

Pitfalls in the Single Life

There are some dangers out there in the single life, some pitfalls you would do well to recognize and avoid. Before we leave this chapter, let's look at those.

1. *Believing lies.* Satan is called the father of lies. His battle strategy whether you are single or married is to deceive and discourage. Here are three of his most well-crafted lies for single people.

- *You are not a whole person unless you are married.*

The debilitating aspect of this lie is that you won't see life beginning for you *until* that person comes along. And if you should become suddenly single again (through death or unwanted divorce), you will return to the life of a person on permanent "injured reserve" status.

● *Only single people are lonely.* Loneliness is part of the human condition. Everyone is lonely at times. When you believe this lie, you bemoan your loneliness and blame it on being single instead of dealing with it as part of the normal process of life.

● *You can't really have a home until you're married.* If you buy this one, you will miss out on the joys of being hospitable now, and you will miss some wonderful ways God wants to provide for you by enabling you to create a home.

2. *Sexual immorality.* This is a major pitfall that has caused absolute devastation in the lives of some people I know. The point is this: God has reserved sexual intercourse for marriage. Sex is necessary to propagate humanity, but it is also given as a gift to soothe, renew, bind, and bring intimacy to a married couple who are committed to handling the joyful and rugged road of marriage and family.

Outside of marriage, God forbids sexual intercourse. And he does so for very good reasons. After watching people who have violated God's design for sex, I have become convinced that outside of marriage, sex becomes addictive behavior because sex is not, as people think, mostly a physical act, but a "whole person" intimacy that affects every level of a person's life. Apart from the security and commitment of a marriage relationship, the intensity of a sexual relationship becomes destructive. God says in his Word that sin enslaves us. That's true in the area of sexual immorality. Where sex within marriage builds, sex outside of marriage destroys.

To be a sexually active single is to be a very lonely, frustrated single. Part of the grace that God gives single people is the strength to be chaste, as difficult as that may be. Remaining chaste (and free from other sexual addictions like pornography, lust, and voyeurism) after years of unhealthy habits may require outside help. Seek out a trained counselor, a support group, or a friend who is willing to check up with you and hold you accountable.

4. *Worshiping singleness.* This attitude lies at the opposite extreme of cursing your singleness. It is important to accept your singleness and to live fully within its parameters. But it is also important not to find your whole identity in "being single." When singles worship their singleness they can communicate a cynicism about marriage in general and a lack of openness to being married themselves in particular. In men this attitude usually comes across as selfishness. In women it often comes across as harshness and a loss of healthy vulnerability.

Married or Not: A Healthy Sense of Identity

Ultimately, to base our deepest sense of identity in any role, relationship, lifestyle, or career will leave us feeling insecure and needy. Every role, relationship, and career can change. A spouse can die. A business can merge and your job can be eliminated. Good health can be lost. Only when we find our identity and wholeness in a relationship with Jesus Christ, who never changes, are we secure to make the major transitions in life. He is the one constant in a changing world. But he is also the constant that can enable us to live abundantly whether married or single, in college or beyond.

God honors marriage. But to him, we are all single individuals as his children. His children may be married or single. If single, it may be for a few years or many. But singleness is not a curse or a paradise any more than marriage is. Singleness provides one set of challenges, options, and privileges. Marriage provides another. God meets us wherever we are and helps us face the challenges with him. That's good news for all of us—married *or* single.

CHAPTER 10

Parents as Peers: A New Phenomenon

When you've spent most of your life being some-one's kid, it's tough to all of a sudden become a peer, an equal with those people. But one of the tasks of being an adult is to become peers with your parents.

For some people that task is easier than for others. Some parents have prepared the way well. They've worked hard at communicating, they've been diligent in helping you become more independent, they've intentionally attempted to set the stage where the three of you (or more in blended families) could be friends. For some people, becoming peers with parents may take a lifetime. Bad communication traits have been ingrained, poor habits have been established, and this equality-with-parents idea is not going to come to fruition quickly.

Here are some suggestions to help you begin that process of viewing your parents as your equal.

1. *Recognize that your parents are people.* Remember that your parents are neither perfect, nor perfectly awful. It's tough to relate to your parents as peers if you see them as perfection personified or on a par with Attila the Hun.

2. *Be thankful for your parents even if they haven't met your expectations of what parents should be.* They may have given you a dysfunctional home. They may have done worse. But look for ways you can thank them. Gratitude and thankfulness are good building blocks for a peer relationship. If you live out of town, drop them a note, write a letter, or call. If you live in the same town, take them out to dinner and thank them for what they've done for you.

3. *If you've been hurt deeply by your parents, forgive them.* This is much easier said than done. You may even need some professional counseling to help you through the hurt and healing. But if you don't forgive, you'll be consumed by bitterness, and not only will your childhood be a disaster, so will your adulthood.

4. *Become financially independent.* As long as your parents are footing the bill for your college education, car payments, gas, or rent, it will be difficult to establish a peer relationship. The parent-child relationship is one of financial support. The peer relationship is not. The sooner you can become financially independent, the better your chances of becoming peers with your parents. Take responsibility for your own life.

5. *Give your parents some time.* After all, they've been parents all of your life. It will take awhile for them to change. Give them a chance.

6. *Give yourself some time.* Mike Neelley says, "For some of us, becoming peers with parents doesn't begin until we reach our thirties because we have not begun to deal with who we are. Since becoming peers with our parents is a long process, it's plain to me that this takes perseverance, hard work, and a willingness to be honest with yourself. A book that has been helpful to me is *Family Ties That Bind* by Dr. Ronald W. Richardson. Becoming peers with our parents is a journey into self-discovery: Who am I? Why do I do the things I do? Am I perpetuating unhealthy family cycles? How do I change? This book has helped me here.

"Becoming peers with our parents is also a big step on our spiritual journeys, because we will discover how much of how we believe God works in our lives is tied up in our perceptions of how our parents worked in our lives."

7. *Talk to your parents and listen to what they have to say.* Dan Ibabao says, "I suspect we'll always be perceived as our parents' legacy, their one and onlys. How do you grow out of this? I've noted that when I've talked to my mom and dad about real-world concerns, such as relationships, housing, taxes, even something like buying my first car, a bridge was built. It was the opportunity to relate to my parents as peers. I sought advice, and in doing so, I stepped further down the path of adulthood. In turn, my mom and dad saw further evidence their son was growing up. It's amazing that talking in an honest, thoughtful manner can help in the transition."

8. *Don't run back to your parents every time something goes wrong.* Go to them for guidance at times, but don't see them as the rescue rangers. Accept responsibility for the successes and failures of your life.

9. *Stay in touch.* Relationships take time and energy, even the relationship with your parents. Make this one of your priorities in life: to keep the new peer relationship with your parents growing.

Living with Your Parents

Sometimes becoming peers with your parents after college graduation can be complicated by a situation you may not have chosen: having to live with your parents again. What then? How do you continue this more adult relationship while you're still living under your parents' roof? And what are the drawbacks?

I've asked Ken Green, a good friend in his mid-twenties, to share his experience. Ken now lives in his own place, but for several years he lived at home while attending graduate school to receive his M.A. in Speech Communication. This is what he has to say about his experience of living at home.

"After graduating from college, having little money, and planning to pursue further education, I decided that moving back into my parents' house was the prudent financial maneuver. I'm glad I did, for it allowed me the emotional and financial support to finish my graduate work quickly. It freed me from the need to work full time in order to pay rent and tuition when scholarships weren't readily available.

"For me, those were the primary benefits, but there were some costs as well. My relationship with my parents was affected by my choice. That was perhaps the most important area impacted by my decision to live at home. I've heard that the greatest gift a child can give his or her parents is to grow up and become their friend. I think in my case, moving back home after college delayed that process. In order to maintain some sense of my own autonomy, which seemed especially dear after living largely free from supervision through college, I cultivated an emotional and relational distance from them that I think they understood but found annoying. I was aware of it at the time but found myself unable or unwilling to change, and though I believe I mentioned it to one of them once, we never discussed it as a family.

"I don't think it caused any real harm to our

relationship, but I do think I might have been able to continue the process of differentiation from them without the strain of maintaining a somewhat artificial distance had I been living on my own.

"My parents were really good about trying to give me as much 'room' as possible. They moved my room downstairs, which helped keep me away from their cigarette smoke (a constant source of irritation and a point of contention since I was old enough to understand the Surgeon General's warnings) as well as providing more separate living quarters. Despite this and their ability to 'leave me alone' much of the time, I found myself avoiding spending time there when possible. I came home after they were in bed when possible, and would leave before they were up or after they were gone for the day. In retrospect, I'm amazed at the lengths that I took to carve out my sense of independence in a situation that seems now not to have demanded it.

"The second area affected by my decision to move back home after college was my maturity and ability to be responsible for financial and related issues. My mom has always been the bookkeeper in the family, and by living at home I was able to continue to rely on her willingness to help me with mundane tasks such as filing income tax returns and filling out and making sense of odious insurance forms. While I was certainly capable of doing these things, it was easy to choose not to since family members tend to fall easily into their traditional roles in their families of origin. By allowing my mom to do many such chores, I feel I deprived myself of certain essential 'adult' responsibilities.

"The third area affected by my move was my self-image. I found myself feeling self-conscious about my living situation, especially around my peers and colleagues at work. I felt a need (when the subject came up) to explain why a twenty-four-year-old would still be living at home.

"It certainly wasn't an entirely negative experience, and I am grateful to both my parents for doing as much as they could to make me comfortable in a situation that I wasn't completely excited about. I think for me the economic benefits made the experience worthwhile; I hope my parents would agree.

"For many people, especially those who are already able to relate to their parents more as fellow adults, I'm sure the experience could be easier and more predominantly positive than I found it to be. My advice would be to air out your agendas early on. Try to be as open with your feelings as possible so as to avoid allowing unnecessary resentment to build up in your living situation."

Ken has shown us some of the difficulties that can arise when you're living at home while attempting to become a peer with your parents. The point is that developmentally all of us need to make the transition from seeing parents as parents only to seeing parents as peers. For some of us, living with our parents will complicate that process. But for all of us, it's important to become peers with our parents as we move beyond college.

CHAPTER 11

Graduate School: The Big Show

Technically, graduate school is not "beyond college." You're still going to classes, doing research, writing papers, spending time in the library, doing homework.

But practically, it's different. You have smaller classes, a closer relationship with the professor, and more work that's probably more difficult as well.

But because graduate school is so similar to what you've already experienced in college and because you've proven yourself as a student, this chapter will be brief. I'll be giving some general insights to help you decide about graduate school and to prepare you for what lies ahead.

Doug Early, who spent a year in graduate school, says, "Balance is the key. Yes, the work load jumps significantly, but so has your ability to learn, your desire to learn (after all, it's what you've chosen), and most of the time, your motivation for finishing the degree. In the year I was at graduate school, I read about a billion more books than in my undergrad days, wrote about a billion more papers (about a billion times longer too), and spent about a billion more hours in the library. Yet, I *never* worked on a Sunday, generally got much more sleep than as an undergrad, spent many a night with friends eating nachos, played basketball every Friday, and watched many hours of TV (usually sports). Almost always, those things that sound like 'wasting time' made the whole experience worth doing. If I had neglected relationships, neglected my health, or for that matter even neglected 'vegging out,' I think my studies would have suffered.

"My advice is to live a full, well-rounded life, and the work will take care of itself. Get a calendar to keep track of assignments, your schedule, and appointments. And remember, this advice is from a college English major who never once wrote a first draft in his undergraduate days and graduated with a 3.4 grade point average. Grad school is the big league, folks. If you don't look ahead on day one and plan, almost precisely, when you will do what, come the last week of class sheer terror will set in, followed by a career at Texaco pumping gas."

I spent some time in graduate school and I agree with Doug. Here are some principles for you to consider as you think about going into the big leagues of graduate school.

1. *Graduate school is tougher than undergraduate school.* It's also more competitive. Every person in that school is there because they chose to apply and because their grades and GRE scores were higher than others. The competition is tougher the higher the league in which you play; the higher rated the school, the more intense the competition. To use a major league baseball expression, graduate school is the "Big Show."

2. *Enter graduate school with an aggressive mind-set.* Realize that graduate school will be tough but that you're qualified and bright or you wouldn't be there. You can compete but you'd better be ready. Get a jump start. Figure out what your assignments are and don't put them off.

3. *Use your study skills and fine-tune them.* You already know how to study. This book doesn't need to deal with that. (However, if you feel your skills are rusty, you might want to pick up another book I've written with this publisher, *How to Survive in College.* I devote several chapters to that subject.)

4. *Live a balanced life.* In graduate school there is always too much to do. You could always research one more resource, write one more page on a test, write another section for a term paper. Don't overdue it. Play that basketball, watch some TV, eat a few nachos. The balanced life will give you the ability to survive the long haul. Graduate school is not a sprint; it's more like a marathon. Living a balanced life will help you survive the long distance.

5. *Don't feel driven to jump immediately into graduate school after earning your undergraduate degree.* My friend Jim Francese, who earned his master's degree in chemical engineering, says, "Graduate school is hard. Some people go to graduate school right from undergrad school, others work first and then go back. Doing the latter can aid greatly in giving one direction, perspective, and dollars too! I worked for an oil company while studying for my B.S. in chemical engineering. I saw what people with a B.S. in chemical engineering did and found that to get the kind of job I wanted, I needed an advanced degree. A year away from school before returning to graduate school can give you the understanding and motivation you need to make the most of your time in graduate school."

My advice to the students I hang out with is don't be in too big a hurry to hit graduate school. If you're already in graduate school, great. If you want to take a break, fine. Because when you get to graduate school, you need to be ready. And the students I know who have spent a year away before entering medical school, law school, or other graduate schools have been helped more than hindered by their year away.

6. *On the other hand, don't wait forever.* As I look back on my life now, I regret jumping immediately into graduate school in psychology. I didn't prepare myself well and my time there wasn't that profitable. But I do regret that I didn't go to seminary when I was in my twenties, after I had worked in a couple of churches. Now I find that if I want to be ordained, a seminary education is a must. And for me to go back to school is more difficult now that I have four children. I would have to give up a wonderful job, curtail a lot of my writing projects, and more. So don't wait forever.

Enough already on graduate school! You're experienced. You're prepared. So let's leave the world of academics and jump into what society calls "the workplace."

CHAPTER 12

Take That Job and ...

I've been out of college for twenty-three years. In that time, I've been a youth director in a church, part-owner and vice president of a company that published material and provided resources for youth workers nationally, an editor of a magazine, a director of operations for a film company, a consultant in the area of fund raising, management, and curriculum development, a writer, a president of a non-profit organization, and a college pastor.

On the other hand, I have a good friend, Ardean Wood, who upon completing graduate school joined the Boeing Corporation. He's been an engineer for Boeing for thirty-four years.

Chances are you will end up in the workplace somewhere between Ardean and me. You'll probably have more than one employer. But you may not be in as many vocational pursuits as I have been.

You've probably just graduated. You've got that diploma in hand. Your family and friends have congratulated you. You've even received a few graduation presents (maybe even this book).

In essence, not only have you graduated, but you've also been kicked out of this world of academia where you've spent so many years in the past. Unless you move on to graduate school, this fall is going to be different from any fall you've ever encountered. (Just think, since pre-school, you've been on an academic schedule. You began school in the fall, took a Christmas break, continued at school, took an Easter break, finished school, and then were on summer vacation.) But not only will the fall be different. So will Monday morning.

You need a job. You need one for several reasons. The most obvious reason is that you need to eat. And God structured this world with the notion that to eat and survive, you need to work. But you also need to work because you want to make a contribution to society, you want to utilize your skills, and you want to do something with your time. So you need to find a job.

And the job you find is important. The bulk of your time other than sleeping is spent on the job and in going to and from work. You want to make that time count, so a job search is important.

How to Find a Job

Where do you start? Doug Early advises, "Look for what *you're* interested in (regardless of résumé, status, or money). And use the contacts you have. Ask around. Most people working in their twenties heard about their job through a friend or relative. I held off on this because I didn't want to impose. I ended up getting a job through a newspaper ad, but I found out that many people I know could and, more importantly, *would* have helped me. Most employers would rather hire a 'known' commodity than some unknown."

So use the contacts you know, and begin the job search process by setting up informational interviews.

If you've never worked in the corporate world or have only touched that world briefly, you need to explore and discover. The informational interview is the way to do that. My friend Stu Harris, who has had three different jobs since he left college, says, "Set up informational interviews with anybody you know in the field in which you're interested. Come prepared with *lots* of questions. When leaving, ask for names. Contact these people and do the same thing. Keep an index card file on everybody you talked with and the date you last spoke with those people. Keep notes on these people and keep in touch. This accomplishes two things: (1) it gives you firsthand information on what these jobs are really like; (2) it gives the employers a chance to meet you in an informal way. They can become your counselors, and they may even hire you."

One place to start with your informational interviews is with people in the church where you've been worshiping during your college years. Most older adults are willing to help college students move into the world of work. And Christians in particular are eager to help younger Christians along. As a college pastor, I want my students to meet Christians in the corporate world, Christians in education, Christians in government, and I'm excited about putting these people together with students. You will probably find the same desire and a similar network in your church.

Another place to get an informational interview is through the placement center at your university. In fact, on our campus, recruiters representing businesses, government agencies, and non-profit corporations are constantly visiting the campus to interview students. Use the recruiters and the resources of your university to set up informational interviews.

My friend Dan Ibabao adds these words about the

informational interview: "First of all, know your objective. Find those companies you truly wish to work in. Then, identify the people in the positions of power to hire you. (You generally want to bypass the personnel office—they process so many résumés, you may get lost in the shuffle.) Write them. Ask for an informational interview. Begin networking with others who are in your field of interest."

Internships: A Bridge to the Workplace

Internships are an excellent way to get your foot in the corporate door. Internships can be utilized while you're still in college or in the first few years after graduation. Dan Ibabao says, "If you're looking for a bridge between academia and the workplace, I've got one for you. I'm a true believer in internships. Many organizations have them. And if you're a bold person, you can approach organizations that don't have one and start one up.

"Internships provide great experiences and a practical way of getting knowledge in a working environment. And, believe me, it's an eye opener! What an opportunity to ride the roller coaster; you'll see the highs, lows, and "hurry up and waits" of your future career. Here's the chance to crank out material, absorb information, make mistakes, and correct them.

"I did my time with an ABC television affiliate in Seattle. For three months I worked for a news magazine show. As one of the sound techs, I got to know my cohorts, picked up the day-to-day knowledge, and even learned a few new tricks! It was a great preview for a prospective career, and certainly did wonders for my résumé.

"Internships provide win/win scenarios for both you

and the company. You get practical on-the-job training. In some cases you get college credits or a small salary. In addition, there may be opportunities to springboard you back into the organization. You also get to work side by side with people who are doing things you hope to do. It's your foot in the door. And the company benefits by receiving needed help in work areas, individuals who know the system and how to work it. When they recruit for full-time placements, they also get known quantities—they are familiar with potential candidates applying for the job openings."

Interviewing

Let's imagine that you have done some informational interviews. You may even have served as an intern. But you still don't have a job. Now comes the serious stuff. Interviewing. Here are some thoughts on that process and what follows.

Stu Harris says, "Give yourself time; don't expect to find a job in the first week. It will most likely take a few months. Make 'looking for a job' a full-time job, but also give yourself a vacation now and then and just go relax."

Bob Regan recommends that you adopt this attitude when you interview: "The most important thing to remember in a job interview is that you are making a trade. You are trading your experience and education and energy for their money. The trade ideally should 'bless both parties.' If it does, you won't need to complain later about what you're being paid, and the company won't have to complain about what they're paying you."

After You Get the Job

So now you have your first (or second or third) beyond-college job. What are some principles for surviving and succeeding in that job? Here are a few that I've culled from twenty-three years in the job market and from talking to a few friends.

1. *Realize that your first job probably won't be your last job.* Don't get too picky about which job you take as your first one. Primarily you need work experience. There is a catch-22 reality in the work force. No experience, no job. No job, no experience. So you need a job or an internship before you can move to the next job. All of us would love to have dozens of employers begging for our services. That probably won't happen. Look around, don't jump at the first job, but don't hang back too long either. A job gives you experience. Experience helps you move up the workplace ladder.

2. *Work hard.* Work smart. Work long when you must but don't become a workaholic. Employers are looking for people who don't mind hard work.

3. *Keep your commitments.* If you say you will do something on the job, do it. Earn trust.

4. *Be organized.* Keep your office and your files in order so you don't waste time digging through piles of paper to find something you need. Keep a calendar handy and keep track of your long-term commitments as well as your day-to-day responsibilities. Look at what's been left undone today and make a plan for dealing with those items tomorrow. Employers appreciate well-organized people.

5. *Know your job.* Learn all you can about your job. Years ago I read a pamphlet by Dr. Norman Vincent Peale. He said if you'd give an hour a day to studying your job and an hour a day to thinking creatively about how to better do your job, within five years you'd be a national expert on that job. I agree with him. I've never followed his advice completely, but I do know that when I've studied and thought creatively about what I'm doing, my effectiveness at work escalates.

6. *Remember, your number-one boss is God.* Work for him. Work hard and smart for your earthly boss, but remember that what really counts is what the Lord thinks about your effort.

7. *Be Christ's ambassador at work.* God will give you some great opportunities to share your faith in a relational way while at work. But be sure that you're walking what you're talking. The best way to "win the right to be heard" is by doing a good job.

8. *Don't overemphasize money; concentrate on contribution.* If you're concentrating on the unique and wholehearted contribution you can make to your company, the money will usually take care of itself.

9. *Be careful about becoming too political in the workplace.* Beware of flattering the boss, stepping on people as you move up the corporate ladder, playing loose with values, gossiping. These tactics will fail in the end.

10. *Don't compromise your morals.* After all, you have to look at yourself in the mirror when you get home.

11. *Do your own job.* Don't worry about what everyone else is doing.

12. *Put others first.* The golden rule, "Do unto others as you would have them do unto you," also works at work.

13. *Don't be surprised or angry when you're treated unfairly.* Life isn't always fair. But if you're "playing to an audience of one"—viewing God as your boss—you can still be a great employee in the midst of inequities.

14. *When it's time to move on, move.* The following advice from Bob Regan should be acted upon after you've been at one job long enough to learn something about the thirteen principles listed above. "I found that if you experience the 'Monday Blues' or 'TGIF's' too much over an extended period of time, then it's time to make a change. I believe that to live a healthy, happy, productive life you need to enjoy your work. To truly be excellent at what you do, you've got to love it." In most cases, it's much better to leave a job after you've found a new one. If you don't, you might find yourself spending some frustrating days in unemployment.

Those are some thoughts about employment. But what about unemployment? What if you can't find a job immediately? Or you find one and then lose it? Or you quit prematurely? Unemployment can be a tremendous burden to some people. Tackling that burden is the subject of the next chapter.

CHAPTER 13

How to Survive Unemployment

When we graduate from college, unemployment is one of the furthest thoughts from our minds. We know we are eminently qualified to be a valuable member of the work force. Companies should be dying to employ us.

Unfortunately, however, unemployment may not be that far from reality. A good percentage of the students I know have a difficult time finding that first job. And sometimes that first job may not be a good fit and they leave and find themselves "in between jobs"—a more antiseptic way of saying "unemployed."

Being unemployed is a very difficult position in which to find yourself. Because work is so equated with worth and with wealth, unemployment makes us feel poor in spirit and poor in pocketbook. Our very identity and sense of self-confidence comes into question when we don't have a job.

I have a talented friend who is facing that situation right now. His name is Peter Larson. Peter is bright, articulate, successful. He graduated from college and in his twenties became a successful journalist writing for major newspapers in Orlando and then in Dallas. While he was in Texas, he had a conversion experience. As a result, he not only recommitted his life to Christ, but also gave up his journalism career to enroll in seminary. Upon graduation from seminary, he married Beth and took a short-term position at a church. That position has ended and he's without work.

I've asked Peter to write his feelings about unemployment. This is his response.

Peter Larson's Story

The Shock of Unemployment

Years ago, as a newspaper reporter in Texas, I was sent out to cover the closing of a steel mill where thousands of workers had lost their jobs.

Without warning, these men had been stripped of their dignity and self-respect. I remember feeling sorry for them. And yet, I couldn't imagine it happening to me. Unemployment was like some rare disease that only happened to other people. Nobody in my hard-working Protestant family had ever been unemployed, and so I felt immune.

Today, I am unemployed. I have been living for five months in my parents' home. My wife is seven months pregnant with our first child. Our bank account has dwindled, and I often wonder if we'll be able to make the next car payment. Meanwhile, I keep interviewing for jobs that seem just out of reach, beyond my grasp.

In my case, unemployment was the result of a career change. After ten years as a newspaper reporter I entered graduate school to prepare for the ministry. Three years later, I was starting out at the entry level in a brand new field. Although I'd been successful as a journalist, I had to prove myself all over again. And I found that many churches were reluctant to hire someone with no track record as a pastor.

How does a person survive unemployment? Without a doubt, this has been the hardest five months of my life.

It's hard to handle rejection from employers, hard to maintain your self-respect. It's hard relating to family and friends, even when they're trying to be supportive. Conversations seem awkward and embarrassed because people don't know what to say or how to help. At church or in the supermarket, people ask the same question: "Have you found a job yet?"

Nothing really prepares you for the shock of unemployment. Most of what we learn in college prepares us to succeed, achieve, and advance in the career world. Nobody teaches classes on failure because nobody expects to fail. And so it's a tremendous blow when you suddenly find yourself out of work or between jobs.

Unemployment strikes at the heart of your dignity and self-respect. So much of our identity is centered around our jobs and careers, where we work, or how much money we earn. When you are unemployed, you almost feel as if you no longer exist. Your identity, your self-definition, have been taken from you.

Recently I filled out an insurance form that asked the question: "Where are you employed?" I had to leave the space blank. And I thought to myself, "That's me—a blank space." When you're unemployed you feel empty and expendable. The working world seems to move on without you, while you sit on the sidelines.

Late at night I find myself wrestling with God, searching for hope and meaning. Sometimes I feel like shouting, "Hey, this isn't supposed to happen to me! I've been to college and graduate school! I've always been honest and hard-working!" Like Job, I find myself asking, "Why me, Lord? Why have I been singled out for suffering?"

But the truth is that most of us will probably be unemployed at some point in life, or at least in transition between jobs or careers. It might be voluntary or involuntary. It might last six days or six months. But unemployment happens to most people—whether we are highly skilled or unskilled, blue collar workers or professionals. I have known many executives who suddenly found themselves "terminated" or "phased out"—another way of saying that they had been fired.

Quite often the process of firing employees is abrupt and dehumanizing. One friend of mine, a newspaper editor, didn't know he'd been fired until he arrived at work one morning and switched on his computer. The computer informed him that his access code was no longer valid—he had been "purged" from the system. I'm sure his supervisor could have softened the blow by telling him in person, beforehand. Instead, he had to learn the news from a machine. My friend felt ashamed and humiliated.

How do people cope with unemployment? I don't have any simple answers or surefire advice. Other people can instruct you how to write a résumé or interview for a job. But during these past few months I've grown closer to God and learned to trust him more. In some ways, these have been the best five months of my life.

The story is told about a Navy captain who called his men together on the eve of D-Day in World War II. The ship was just about to cross the English Channel and face the fury of German artillery. Knowing this, the captain tried to encourage his troops. "Men," he said, "I know a lot of you are feeling anxious and afraid. But when you think about it, fear is a very healthy thing."

Just then a seaman spoke up, "Captain, if what you say is true, I'm the healthiest man in the entire Navy!"

Unemployment is frightening. But I also believe that it's God's way of inviting us into a healthier, stronger relationship with him. God wants to stretch our faith to new limits. But most of all, God wants to teach us grace. When my strength fails, when I feel frightened about the future, I hear God saying, "My grace is sufficient for you, for my power is made perfect in weakness" (2 Corinthians 12:9).

The Guilt Trap

When you're unemployed, it's easy to believe that God is angry with you. You might feel rejected and abandoned, as if God has singled you out for punishment. When this happens, you are sinking into the guilt trap.

Jesus never promised us a life without pain and suffering. Far from it! Jesus warned his disciples that they would face all sorts of hardships and trials. It's a mistake to believe that "good people" don't suffer, or that "good Christians" are never unemployed.

As Christians, we shouldn't be surprised when life doesn't go smoothly. All of us will encounter suffering. The apostle Peter offers this advice, "Dear friends, do not be surprised at the painful trial you are suffering, as though something strange were happening to you" (1 Peter 4:12).

Who's Your Boss?

Have you ever worked for a company where you had many supervisors and managers giving orders? It's confusing. Unless you figure out who really is your boss it is impossible to set priorities.

As believers, we work for God. Whether we sell insurance or perform brain surgery, the best of our skill and energy is committed to the kingdom of God. Christ has important work for every one of us, no matter what profession we choose. And until we discover Christ, we will not find our true calling, our true "vocation."

In Christ we discover our true calling. We are called to care passionately about the world, to serve Christ, and to love men and women into the kingdom of God. Whatever we do for a living, this is our job.

If God is our employer, then there is always work for us to do. On this very day that I write these words, this is what God has for me: He wants me to love my wife, write a letter, volunteer to move furniture at the church, and baby-sit for my sister-in-law. This work might seem trivial. But in God's eyes, it has eternal significance.

We are employees of God. With him, we are never out of work.

Where Does It Hurt?

Faith isn't a pain killer. It doesn't take away the sting of rejection or the fear of unpaid bills. At times, my own emotions have ranged from despair to anger. But I've learned that God can handle my emotions. I can't fake it with him, and so it's pointless to pretend that I'm not hurting. It's okay to admit I'm discouraged or depressed.

It's also important for me to be emotionally honest with my wife, Beth. Otherwise I bottle up a lot of anger and rage. If an interview goes badly or a check bounces, it's good to get those feelings out in the open before they explode somewhere else.

Some Christians believe it isn't "spiritual" to have these emotions. They believe that you should never feel hopeless or depressed. So you end up feeling even more depressed and guilty, because, by their definition, you are a lousy Christian.

But the Bible talks about a God who can handle our deepest pain and our ugliest emotions. We don't have to fake it with God, and we don't have to feel ashamed or afraid to share our true emotions.

Last week, I went to a doctor to be treated for hemorrhoids. Trying to describe my symptoms was embarrassing. But the doctor listened to my complaints in graphic detail. It would have been pointless to pretend I wasn't hurting.

Jesus is the great physician who is eager to hear our problems. He came to help the sick, not the healthy (Luke 5:31).

I love the story of blind Bartimaeus, found in the Gospel of Mark. Bartimaeus is sitting on a road outside Jericho when he learns that Jesus is passing nearby. So he begins screaming, "Jesus, Son of David, have mercy on me!" Offended by the noise, the crowd tells him to be quiet. But the Bible says that Bartimaeus "shouted all the more." At last, Jesus hears Bartimaeus and heals him saying, "Your faith has healed you" (Mark 10:46–52).

Sometimes, faith is screaming for help at the top of your lungs! When my wife and I feel hurt or hopeless, we take it to God in prayer. Jesus isn't offended! He hears us and heals us.

Don't Panic

God knows your needs. He knows your Visa bill and your bank balance and every penny you owe on your student loans. God knows exactly what you need to survive, even better than you do!

I've been amazed at the way God has provided for me during the past five months. I left my last job with no money in the bank—absolute zero. Since then, we have received more than $5,000 in gifts from friends in the church where I used to work! All of these gifts have been anonymous from people who know us and care about us.

Usually, we have received money the same day some bill was due. Last month, when it looked like we wouldn't be able to pay some major bills, we received $1,500 in one day. God seems to know exactly when we need money, and exactly how much. We pray about our needs and God answers.

Of course, we're not living in luxury. We've been staying in my parents' basement and sharing most of our meals with them. But God has provided enough money to pay our basic bills, with even a little left over for fun and frills.

Whatever money we receive, Beth and I give at least 10 percent back to God. Recently, when I sold my used Jeep for $2,500, I gave 10 percent of that income to the Lord's work. It's risky, tithing when you're unemployed. But the gifts that are really pleasing to God are the gifts that we cannot afford to give.

God can meet your needs. This might sound impractical or even irresponsible. But as a Christian businessman once told me, "God isn't stupid."

Endurance First, Speed Later

Everyone wants to be a winner. We want to be in the "fast lane" and the "fast track," sprinting from success to success. So what happens when you're stuck on the sidelines?

I came across this quote recently in the "Runner's Log," the calendar where I record my daily running time and distance: "The training gospel: endurance first, speed later."

In every sport, the first step is building endurance. Great athletes are usually the ones who train the hardest, not just those with natural ability. I learned this the hard way last summer when I climbed 14,000 feet to the top of Mount Rainier. The leader of our expedition warned me that I should train hard for several months for the climb. But instead, I relied on my own strength and stamina. I made it to the top—but it nearly killed me. I didn't have the endurance needed for high-altitude climbing.

God isn't impressed with speed. He wants to teach us endurance. In the agony of unemployment, God has improved my stamina and strength and endurance. My pain isn't pointless: it's God's way of training me for the hard races ahead. Paul offers this advice in his letter to the Romans: "We also rejoice in our sufferings, because we know that suffering produces perseverance; perseverance, character; and character, hope" (Romans 5:3).

When God wanted to train the people of Israel, he often took them out into the wilderness. In the desert, they learned to trust God in the harshest possible environment. Abraham, Moses, Joshua, and John the Baptist were desert graduates.

Unemployment has been a desert experience for me. In this harsh environment of failure and rejection, God teaches me lessons of endurance, courage, and hope. I have lost my fear of unemployment; I have lost my fear of failing. I have learned to keep running when there are no cheering crowds, when only God is watching.

Endurance first, speed later!

Earning Grace or Learning Grace

"Free gift!"

Those two words fill me with suspicion! I have learned to mistrust salespeople when they offer free jewelry, free vacations, and free studio portraits. Usually, those gifts turn out to be worthless, and they aren't free at all. There is no such thing as a free gift in our society.

But it's a mistake to apply this same logic to God. God's grace is a free gift—no strings attached. You cannot earn or deserve his grace. The heart of the Christian life is not based on human performance, achievement, success, service, or striving. The heart of the Christian life is receiving the free grace of God, the kind of grace that is poured out exactly when we don't deserve it, when we have nothing to give in return.

All my life, I've been strong, self-reliant, and self-confident. I have worked hard for everything I have received. I enjoyed helping other people, but I dreaded the thought of receiving help. I have lived too much by human strength, rather than by grace. When I was employed and productive, it was easy to feel that God was indebted to me.

God has used unemployment to teach me grace. I am getting better, I hope, at receiving free gifts. I have been surprised to discover that Christians still love me even when I have no way of earning their love. One friend invited me to a Seattle Seahawks game. Others have invited us to dinner. Dozens of people tell me that they pray for us every day.

Last week, after a difficult day, I received a letter from a college freshman who used to be in my Sunday school class. I hadn't heard from her in years. The letter ended with these words: "You have made an impact on my life, and I will never forget you. I know that you are probably extremely busy, but I would love to hear about your life, and Beth's, too. I miss you very much!"

With this letter, God poured out grace on me. At a time when I felt worthless, God used this letter to comfort me. It was a free gift, totally unexpected and undeserved.

Soon I will be employed again. Since I started this chapter I have received an offer of work. It looks like my journey in the desert is finally over. I only hope that I remain close to God and that I continue learning grace, not attempting to earn it.

Pain and Potential

Peter Larson has painted the picture well, showing us the pain involved in unemployment, as well as the unexpected potential one finds to experience God's grace.

Doug Early also went through a time of unemployment recently. Here's what he adds: "I was unemployed for three months. During that time I began wondering if I truly was as big a loser as everyone else obviously thought I was. The only thing that kept me going was some volunteer work as an ESL (English as a second language) tutor. There, I *knew* I was good and I loved teaching. It gave me reassurance and self-esteem. Even if you're not paid and can't do it very often, keep your hand in something you're good at. And let people affirm you—you may need it further down the road."

Let me summarize briefly the main points you'll need to consider when you are coping with a period of unemployment.

1. *Cling tightly to God.* In the midst of unemployment, you especially need God's support. When you pray, ask him not only for a job, but also to reveal to you what he wants to teach you in this period of your life.

2. *Treat your job search as a full-time job.* Remember: your work is "looking for work." Keep searching, applying, and interviewing even if the "no's" seem almost overwhelming.

3. *Continue to do the things you do well.* Bolster your self-confidence and remind yourself of your talents and skills by using those skills even while you're unemployed.

4. *Treat the extra time you have as a gift.* Take care of unfinished business, clean out your files, finish a letter or book, and prepare yourself for your next job.

Unemployment is very difficult, but it can also be a time of great growth. See the potential as well as the pain in this (hopefully) short chapter of your life.

CHAPTER 14

$$$hh, We're Talking Money Here

What color is money?

Red? Because it inflames the passions of so many as they pursue the almighty dollar? Ice blue—for the coolness money can convey as you bomb around town in your new BMW? How about green, for the envy it produces in others? Could it even be white—because it really is neutral and what you do with it determines its value? Or is it brown—dirty, so it contaminates whatever it touches? Maybe to you money is just gray—murky and confusing.

Regardless of its color, money matters. We live in a society dominated by money. We *need* money. As Jackie Mason used to say, "I have enough money to last me the rest of my life—unless I buy something."

As you move beyond college, you're entering a world of ever-widening choices and ever-increasing temptations that result from having, not having, wanting, and managing money. You're emerging from the halls of academia into the malls of the commercial world, and there's a whole new set of challenges to face.

Discussions about money can be theoretical; they can

also be intensely practical. This chapter will attempt to cover both theory and practice. Here are some principles for thinking about and using the green stuff.

Rule #1: Money Is a Dream; Money Is a Nightmare

To some extent, almost all of us at one time or another buy into the world's dream that money equals success and that more money can buy the elusive happiness we are currently missing. Unfortunately for us dreamers, the dream can quickly become a nightmare.

It is wonderfully affirming to go out into the workplace with your unique gifts and talents and get paid for doing what you love to do and have been educated or trained to do. But, if the affirmation of getting paid for services rendered results in your finding your identity in that job—or worse, in that paycheck—nightmares can result.

The truth is that true happiness and self-worth can't be found in your bank balance. J. Paul Getty achieved status and fame as the "world's richest man." But he died a lonely and bitter individual. Once he was asked, "How much money will make you happy?" His reply was, "One dollar more."

Bruce Bailey, a friend of mine who just turned fifty, has been in the work force since he was nineteen, as a creator and designer. I admire him as someone who has managed his money well. He says, "If we chase the mythical pot of gold at the end of the rainbow for its own sake, the rainbow keeps moving away. If, on the other hand, we simply strive to make full use of our unique treasure house of God-given gifts, talents, and skills where they are needed, money will tend to find us. Excellence is the result. And long-term excellence almost always gets rewarded."

Rule #2: What You Think You Own, Really Owns You

This rule could be entitled "The J. Paul Getty Rule." When you have a lot of wealth, you think you need one dollar more. When you have something to lose, you think about losing it. When you bet your life on money, you become uncomfortable, and you're not even sure why. But the resulting drive and abiding feeling often is this: a creeping sense of dissatisfaction and a craving for more. You're owned and controlled by what you desire to own and control.

Rule #3: Money Has Its Own Rules and Terms; Be Knowledgeable

I can't take the time in this book to go over all the rules of finance. I also don't have the expertise to do so. But topics like interest, arbitrage, collateral, equities, balance sheets, and bottom lines are financial topics with rules. If you're moving into the world of finance, development, and banking, you need to become an expert. And even if you're simply going to be a person who makes some money, balances a checkbook, and goes about life without much financial clout, the rules of money are still important. Spend some time learning the terms and the rules.

Frankly, I have not been as astute in money matters as I would have liked. I took two courses in economics in college, but I've forgotten most of what I learned. As I've moved through life, I've recognized the fact that having more knowledge in this area would have helped me become a better steward of my resources. I'm trying to correct my deficiencies now. I heartily encourage you to start earlier than I did.

Rule #4: Money Has No Morals

No matter what your Aunt Doris said, money is not the root of all evil. What Paul really said to Timothy in the New Testament is "the *love* of money is a root of all kinds of evil" (1 Timothy 6:10). Money is simply a tool, an inert medium of exchange for goods and services. It is our *attitude* toward money that can get us into trouble.

Bruce Bailey says, "Do an attitude check when you begin to suspect you might be starting to be 'conformed to this world' instead of being 'transformed by the renewing of your mind. Then you will be able to test and approve what God's will is—his good, pleasing and perfect will' (Romans 12:2). You'll notice your attitude growing unhealthy when the products that are advertised begin to look like *necessary additions* to your lifestyle instead of *mere options*."

Rule #5: Give Right to Live Right

What do you think of this financial priority list?

1. Living expenses
2. Savings and investments
3. Giving

Seems pretty practical, doesn't it? Everybody has to take care of their rent and their food and their bills first. Then, if there's a little left over, we try to save a few dollars for next Christmas or to replace the '78 Corolla.

And finally, of course, we take care of our giving to the Lord's work and other charitable causes.

The only problem with this model is that as popular and pragmatic as it may seem, it's wrong. It's not biblical.

God's way, according to Scripture, is reversed from the order we just examined.

1. Giving
2. Living (while saving)

Here's what the Bible has to say about giving.

1. *Give off the top.* Don't wait until you've paid all your bills and gone out to eat to celebrate the payment of your bills before you give to the Lord. Instead, give *first.* Giving off the top stretches our confidence in God. We begin to understand his ownership of all we have. Sometimes it's easier to talk about being a "first fruits" giver than it is to do it, but that's the exercise of faith that produces growth.

2. *Give generously, hilariously, secretly, and sacrificially.* How much should I give? That's a question many of us want answered. Fortunately or unfortunately, there's not a simple answer to that question.

In the Old Testament, tithing was required. A tithe was a tenth—ten percent. But there were other opportunities for giving in Old Testament times, such as feast days. Some biblical scholars have estimated that Old Testament people gave a total of 22 percent of their income.

Our New Testament model is not specific on "how much," but it is on "how." We are to give generously, purposefully, secretly, hilariously, and sacrificially. I've read of businessmen and women like J.C. Penney and R.G. LeTourneau, who have given 90 percent of their income joyfully and lived thankfully on 10 percent.

So if you asked me the question, "How much should I give?" I'd answer, "Somewhere between 10 percent and 99 percent of your income!" But I'd also add, "Give only what you can give cheerfully." The Bible says that God loves a cheerful giver. I have seen cheerful givers and cheerless ones. I have seen people who always try to "do more" to the point where they do not even take care of the needs of their families. They are poor stewards even though they "give until it hurts." I have also seen guilt-ridden givers who feel they can buy their relationship with Jesus Christ. Both types of giving are not in keeping with what the Bible portrays the healthy, generous, cheerful giver to be.

I personally haven't had much of a problem being a willing giver. I attribute that to a decision I made as a grade school student when I foolishly (or so it seemed) promised my whole summer's wages in berry-picking money to an itinerant evangelist who was passing through town. It may not have been a wise investment, but it did "loosen" me up to be a willing giver. God has always taken good care of me, and I am convinced that giving is a wonderful act of worship.

Rule #6: Save as Well as Spend

In life, unexpected things happen. We need to plan for contingencies like illness and schooling and braces and transmissions and roofs and recreation and retirement. Those kinds of contingencies require that we have some kind of savings plan.

Bruce Bailey says, "Don't presume on God's gracious character to get you through some financial emergency when it is his gracious character that gives you the wisdom and ability to plan ahead.

"Another good reason to have a savings and investment plan is to stay out of the habit of borrowing. Hope deferred may make the heart sick, but it certainly helps avoid the rampant abuse of the 'I've got to have it now' debt mentality.

"After you fulfill your planned and proportionate giving to the Lord, then the next layer off the top is for savings. Make some ambitious savings goals. Work toward a regular and increasing percentage until you can save 7–10 percent of your earnings. Don't spend your savings except for items on a list you make that should include an emergency living fund of three to six months income; medical emergencies not covered by insurance; home and retirement needs; continuing education; family planning such as the children's education; automobile replacement; and vacation."

Dan Ibabao also encourages us to "Save, invest, and save! I wish I did when I was younger. Even now, saving is a challenge. It takes discipline, sacrifice, and knowing the buck saved is going to a greater good.

"Many of us are guilty of wanting it *now*. You know, the immediate gratification scenario. 'I saw it hanging on the rack and it was calling out to me.' Forty bucks later, you're wondering, 'Why did I do this?'

"I have to remind myself that I don't need everything that's in front of me. It doesn't mean that I deny myself everything. It does mean knowing my limits. It helps me to write down on a sheet of paper what my expenses are, and what funds are available. It really helps seeing it in black and white."

As part of savings and investment, get good advice. Don't invest in "get-rich-quick schemes." Be conservative and find qualified counsel. Your goals for a return on your money should be attuned to how much risk you can comfortably handle. Your investment counselor can help you analyze the risks of various investments. Historically, a low risk investment is U.S. Government Treasury bills. Bonds are also considered a more conservative investment. Common stocks are somewhat riskier. But probably the best investment you'll ever make is your home. We'll cover the subject of investing in a home in the next chapter.

Rule #7: Live on What You Earn

The first step in living on what you earn is to formulate a budget. You can get budget forms from your local stationery store or you can buy a software package to run on your computer that will help you in budgeting. But whether you use a manual method or a software program the point is: Develop a budget. A budget is simply a tool where you estimate what your income will be, and consequently, what you can spend each week or month. As you earn your income and meet your expenses, you write down income and outgo to see if you're keeping on track. If you're overspending, you pull back. You also make budgeting adjustments as income changes and new needs arise.

As you develop your budgeting process, make sure you have the following line items:

Income (sources both annually and monthly)

Expenses
    giving (church, other ministries, other charities)
    taxes (federal, state, city, property)
    savings (pensions, stocks, cash, bonds)
    housing
    insurance (health, car, life, fire)
    repairs/maintenance
    utilities
    phone

furniture budget
food (groceries and eating out)
clothing (purchases and cleaning)
entertainment and recreation (health club dues,
    dates)
vacation
transportation (auto payments, fuel, repairs and
    maintenance, insurance, tolls, public transporta-
    tion, parking)
gifts
child care
personal (hair stylist)
other obligations (debt reduction)
miscellaneous

Whatever type of form you use, make sure that you can easily *see* budget excesses and shortages.

Here are some more budgeting hints.

1. *Keep the budget simple.* In the beginning, keep your system simple so it won't overwhelm and frustrate you. Later, once you've grown used to the process of budgeting, you can make it more sophisticated.

2. *Discuss the budget with your spouse.* If you're married, make sure you and your spouse are in as much agreement as possible about how to spend what the two of you earn.

3. *Be flexible.* You control the budget; don't let it control you.

Rule #8: Beware of Borrowing
(The Perils of Plastic)

Let's take a look at one more money issue that impacts us: borrowing and credit. Here are two principles:

1. *It is better not to borrow, but some borrowing may be* *necessary*. It would be wonderful if you could pay cash for everything. Unfortunately, most of us can't. Most of us can't buy a house with cash, or even a car. And many of us can't finance graduate school without a loan. The key point is this: don't borrow frivolously. Borrow only on those higher ticket items where borrowing is necessary and then borrow only what you need. Make the highest down payment you can (unless your investment counselor advises otherwise on the basis of tax advantages). And make your monthly payments promptly.

2. *Be careful with credit cards.* Dan Ibabao says, "Beware the credit card crunch. Like chips used in gambling houses, you can't visualize the amount of *money* slipping through your fingers every time you use the plastic. I've seen too many stories of card abuse, where people are in debt for $50,000! You've got to hold yourself accountable. Pay off your bill as soon as possible. Your credit history will look healthier too!"

In addition to what Dan says, I want to add that you should view your card as a cash card (a convenient way to make a purchase) rather than a credit card (that puts you in debt). With a cash card, you pay off the total amount each month. Most credit card companies charge between 15 percent and 21 percent in interest. You don't want to make those kind of payments.

In summary, I'd like to give Bob Regan the final word. Bob is a real estate developer in his late twenties. He spends a lot of his day thinking about money. This is what he says, "The issue of money is not that different from the issue of success. The first question that needs to be addressed is the *purpose* of money. Is money to be used by us to serve ourselves, or to serve God? I believe you were born at this *time* in this *place* for a *purpose*. Our capital-producing capacities are for

God's purpose in furthering his kingdom on earth. Earning money to manage for God is only part of our responsibility. Keeping it productive is the other. Here are my hallmarks for responsible money management: (1) cut consumer debt; (2) save; (3) fund your retirement plan every year; and (4) give as much as you cheerfully can."

You've heard from a few people regarding responsible money management. My suggestion to you is to build your own set of principles right now, then trust God to help you live them out as you manage the resources he's given you.

Now let's move to one of the highest ticket items where you'll ever invest your money: your home. Buying a house is the subject of the next chapter.

CHAPTER 15

Coming Home: The Big Purchase

When you're in college, your purchases usually range from $1 (an ice cream cone) to $10,000 (a car). That's it. You may invest a couple thousand on an engagement ring, but generally purchases are in the lower range.

Then you move beyond college. Time passes and you plan to buy your first house. It's not $1. It's not $10,000. It's $75,000 or $100,000 or $125,000. Your purchase is now a *major* one. You have gone ten times or more over your previous high! That's a significant increase.

Because the process of buying a house is so significant and so emotional (ask any person who has shopped for a house, made the purchase, and paid the thousands of dollars in closing costs!), this chapter is going to be long and detailed. I hope that this chapter not only will teach you how to shop for and buy a home, but that it will also save you thousands of dollars by helping you to buy wisely and well.

So here it is. Almost everything you'd ever want to know about buying your first home. But let's begin with a question that comes even before you learn how to buy a house.

Should I Rent or Buy?

Most of the decision of home buying depends upon where you live. Some areas are "hot," meaning homes are appreciating rapidly and selling quickly. Some are "slow," meaning that it takes awhile to sell your home and houses are not appreciating very quickly. The average appreciation rate for houses in the United States at the time this book was written was 5 percent a year.

With those facts in mind, you need to study your area to see if houses there are appreciating at that rate or not. When you know the appreciation rate (how much houses are going up in value per year), then you can proceed.

1. *Buying in an average market.* What if you live in an average area where houses are appreciating at 5 percent a year and take one to three months to sell?

Should you buy or rent in an average area? Consider this: if a home is going up at 5 percent a year, that would mean on a $100,000 home, the price is going up $5,000 a year. On top of that, if you owned your home you would be gaining equity and have one of the solid tax write-offs that the government allows.

Another issue to consider is how long you plan to live in your home. It pays to buy in an average area if you can live in the house for five years or more. The first year you purchase the home, most of your mortgage payments go directly into interest. So you don't gain much equity unless you can live in the house for at least five years. If you don't have a steady job or are not sure if you like the area you are now living in, it probably isn't right for you to buy a home just yet.

On the other hand, if you know you'll probably be around for at least five years, there is no doubt that a home purchased in an "average" area will be a great investment for you.

2. *Buying in a hot market.* What if you live in a hot area where the houses are being sold in anywhere from one day to two weeks and the homes are appreciating 1–2 percent a month or 12–24 percent a year?

In this market, if you were to buy a home for $100,000, it would go up in price $1,000–$2,000 per month. If you live in this type of area, you should definitely buy instead of rent and buy as quickly as possible. Unless you can save more than $1,000–$2,000 per month, you are losing money every month that you put this decision off. It doesn't even matter if you don't plan to stay in the area long. If you can stay in the house at least one year, the worst you will do is make 12 percent on your money, which is better than most other investments.

And you don't need to be tremendously picky about the house you choose in this type of market. The best plan is just to get in a home and let that home appreciate at the same rate as all the other homes in that market. Then you can take the time to find your "ideal home" *while* you are gaining equity in the "not-so-ideal home" you've purchased.

The best plan for buying a home in a hot area is to follow the suggestions listed in the next few pages of this chapter, but I'd like to add one other point to the strategy: buy the Friday edition of the paper on Thursday night, look over the homes that interest you, and make an appointment on Thursday night to see the home at lunch on Friday. A good priced home in a hot area can be sold in as little as twenty-four hours. You can't hesitate much in a hot market. You need to make finding a home a second job for a while. If you're lucky, your employer will be understanding.

And remember, even in a hot area, location is still important. Some areas are appreciating faster than others, which means you will be making more on your money at a faster rate if you concentrate on location. This will also be helpful when you sell this home to purchase your "dream home." If you can find your dream home a little further away from the extremely hot area, you can get a bigger home for your money because of what you made on your first home in the hot area. Ask your real estate agent which areas of the community in which you live are appreciating the fastest.

3. *Buying in a flat market.* What if you live in a flat market where homes are appreciating only 1–3 percent a year (or not at all) and it takes six months or more to sell your home?

This might be a time when you want to rent. It all depends on how long you are planning to stay in the area. If you are planning to be there for some time and raise your children, then buying a house makes sense, because for most people, owning a home is more enjoyable than renting one. When you own you can do whatever you want to your property and you are still getting the tax benefits. However, if you have a temporary job or you are new to the area, renting might be wise. There are too many horror stories of people buying a home in a flat area, then having to move quickly because of a job change. They end up making double house payments for more than a year as they pay for their new home and also their other home in the flat market area. Think very carefully about making a purchase here.

Arranging a Loan

After you've examined the housing market and decided to buy a house, you need to decide how much you can afford to pay. That's extremely important. A general rule is that if the interest rate is at 10 percent , your house payment is going to be 10 percent of the purchase price. In other words, if you purchase an $80,000 home, your house payment each month is going to be around $800 a month, which includes real estate taxes and home owner's insurance. You will benefit as a home owner on your income taxes, and you will make around $4,000 a year in appreciation, but basically you will write a check for $800 every month. Can you afford $800 now? Will you be able to afford it when you have children? If not, maybe you should look for houses in a slightly lower range.

Pete Shimer, a Certified Public Accountant in his late twenties who bought his first home last year, says, "The realities of today's economics are that almost all of us will need some financial support to buy a house. This usually comes in the form of a down payment that some relative is willing to help you with. It is important to get this subject out of the way at the start. How much is being given? And what are the terms or conditions, if any, for repayment?"

It's good to know if you have help in the down payment process. But whether you do or don't, the next step is to go to a lending institution to determine what they say you can afford.

The best way to know exactly what you can afford is to get pre-approved for a loan with a financial institution. For instance, if you cannot get approved for a $100,000 loan by most banks because you don't qualify, it doesn't really matter what you *feel* you can afford.

When you're working on a loan, don't go to only one lender. Check on five to ten different loan institutions to find who offers the best rate at the least amount of cost. What this means is that if Bank A offers to give you a loan at 10.5 percent and it will cost you nothing for the loan, this might be a better deal than Bank B who offers you a loan at 10 percent but charges you 5 points to get the loan. A "point" is just another term for percentage. Each point will cost you 1 percent of the price of the house. In other words, if you want to buy a $100,000 home, it will cost you $1,000 per point.

When you go to a financial institution don't just ask them at what percentage you can get your loan, but also ask how many points they are charging and then crunch some numbers. (If you're not a good numbers cruncher, meet with one of your friends who was an accounting major in college or one who is in banking or real estate, or go to a member of your family who understands.) Remember that, on the average, each half a percent you can get your loan down means $50 off your house payment each month. Ask yourself, am I willing to go for Bank B's 10 percent loan, which will cost $5,000 in points now, but will lower my house payment for thirty years by $50 a month? Or do I want the 10.5 percent loan that will cost me nothing in points now but will cost me $50 per month for the next thirty years? And don't forget that points are not the only thing you will pay for when purchasing a house. You also have to make a down payment, which varies between 3–5 percent (the greater the down payment, however, the less you will have to finance) and closing costs (what the bank charges you for processing the loan), which are also between 3–5 percent . Without paying any points, you will have to shell out $6,000–$10,000 on a $100,000 home. Those costs can sometimes take a bit of the joy out of a first home, especially if you weren't anticipating them.

Once you choose the financial institution with whom you want to do business, that institution will look at your combined income if you're married (or just your income if you're single) and your savings and debt. Then they will report to you the amount they will loan you. This is called *pre-approval*. This does not mean, however, that they will definitely loan you that money. Pre-approval is simply a guess by the loan officer, although they do give fairly accurate estimates. How can you get approved for a loan? Here are some things that will help.

- Buy a house for less than what your pre-approved loan is.
- Pay off all your credit cards, school loans, and car payments, as they will count against you.
- Stay at the same job for two years. This is very important.
- Don't pay any of your bills (including rent or credit cards) late. Late payments affect your credit rating, and a credit rating is carefully considered by your lender.

Choosing a Real Estate Agent

Once you have decided what price of house you can afford, the next step is to decide on a real estate agent. And, by all means, use a real estate agent. It does not cost you, the buyer, one dime to utilize the services of a real estate agent. His or her commission comes from the sale price of the house. In other words, the seller pays the agent; the buyer does not.

Reputable real estate agents know the market and what's on the market. Most have access to a computer that shows them each day which new homes are available. Another bonus in using an agent is that they use their car and their gas to take you around to see the houses. (With what a home will cost you, you need all the savings you can get!)

Lisa Kragerud and her husband Eric have purchased three different homes in their twenties. Lisa says this about real estate agents: "There are some good real estate agents, and there are some real turkeys. At the beginning you might want to use two or three and then narrow it down to the one who is giving you the best service. Be honest with each agent and let them know you are doing this. It will help them to work for you a little harder."

Lisa then lists what she avoids when selecting an agent.

1. *Do they select homes for you to look at that are above your price range?* Immediately dump an agent that tries to go above your means. They are thinking too much about their commission and not enough about your needs.

2. *Do they waste your time?* If they keep taking you to split levels when you've indicated you don't want a split level, if they take days to return your calls, if they drive you to areas where you don't want to live, look for someone else.

3. *Do they intimidate you?* If you don't feel comfortable enough with them to tell them that every house they've shown you is ugly, you may want another agent. Be sure you have agents that make you feel like you can tell them exactly how you're feeling about each house and their service.

Once you've selected your real estate agent, have the agent take you to as many houses in your desired price range as possible. Then, based on what you've seen, *narrow it down to one area of town in which you'd like to live.* The reason I suggest looking in many different areas first is that the same house can cost $20,000 less only ten miles away. Maybe you will decide it's worth a fifteen minute longer commute each day to get a home that is twice as big or half as expensive.

One of the rules as to whether size or location is more important to you is how long you are planning to stay in the house. If five years is your projected limit, location is probably more important. If you want to raise your kids in the house, size is probably a better consideration.

When you've decided the area in which you want to live, look at as many houses as possible so you can get an idea of what style of house you want and what looks like a good deal in that area. People sell their houses for many different reasons, and some people sell their houses under the market (which means they are underpriced) because they are in a hurry to move or they've never studied what a house like theirs is worth.

Try not to get too emotional about the first house you see. You really need to see many houses in your price range before you can figure out just how great a house you can get for the price.

The number-one item to look for in buying a house is *resale value.* You may think you're going to be in this house forever, but you probably won't. I have owned three homes prior to the home I'm buying now. Lisa Kragerud and Eric have had two they've lived in and one they're using as an investment. With that in mind, look for a home that you could sell at a profit in the shortest amount of time. Some things to look for are

1. *Neighborhood.* The three most important rules for resale are location, location, and location. In other words, the neighborhood is the most important factor in resale. And when you look at a home in a particular neighborhood, remember, it is better to buy the least expensive home in the neighborhood than the most expensive home there.

2. *Size of lot.* Buy a home that has a decent yard size. You may want to remodel in the future and you may need the room. And yard size interests people with children who may want to buy your home later.

3. *Age.* Buying a newer home means you will have to spend less money on expensive items like carpeting and you will not have to worry as much about plumbing and electric repairs. The negatives of buying a new home, however, are having to invest in window coverings and landscaping, both of which can be very expensive.

4. *Style.* There are basically four types of homes: the rambler, split-level, tri-level, and two-story. Ramblers with finished basements are called daylight ramblers, but they are basically grouped in the category of two-stories. The style is important in resale. For instance, in the Pacific Northwest split-levels (as you enter the home, you have stairs that lead up and down) have lower resale value because there is an overabundance of them. Most buyers would prefer a home that is different from what everyone else is living in. For that reason, split-levels do not appreciate as much in the Pacific Northwest as other houses do. In other areas of the country, the rambler may be less popular or the two-story may be in temporary disfavor. Find out which kind of house in your area is the one that appreciates the least and stay away from that one if at all possible.

5. *Number of rooms.* It is much easier to resell a three-bedroom home than it is a two. When you buy a two-bedroom home you are limiting yourself to other buyers who are childless, have only one child, or have children living away. You will find it much easier and faster to sell your house if it has at least three bedrooms. Another thing to consider is a family room. Family rooms help the resale value of a home.

6. *School district.* To families with children, the reputation of the school district is critical when buying a home. Even if you are a single person buying your first home and have only vague thoughts of children and teachers, consider the school district. It will help your resale opportunities.

7. *Accessibility.* If you are in a metropolitan area, it's important to have access to the highways as long as the neighborhood is still good. Another consideration is how near the home is to supermarkets and shopping malls.

8. *Extras.* Not only will little extras sell your house more quickly and for a better price, but it is more pleasurable to live in a home with them. Some extras that really count are: gas heat, hardwood floors, vaulted ceilings, sunken living rooms, and unfinished basements. Items like hot tubs and tennis courts are not going to make a house appreciate more than a house without them, and they are very expensive to put in. Don't put them in if you're planning to move in five years.

After you've thought about what you value in a home and an area, look around at many different homes and find one that meets most of your needs. (You'll probably never find a home that meets all your needs; house buying, like life, involves some compromise.) Then make an offer.

Peter Shimer gives this advice. "Be *patiently aggressive!* Patient with the process and the progress; aggressive with opportunity."

Pete continues, "Don't buy the first house you see; be patient. Don't get discouraged when the process is slow. The right opportunity is out there. I looked at over eighty houses during a three-month period before finding my first house! It was worth the wait, though. The house appreciated $40,000 in the first seven months I owned it. Part of the increase had to do with the overall real estate market, but a lot resulted from the fact that it was undervalued when I bought it. The process of looking at eighty other houses was invaluable in finding this gem. Hunt for those bargains; they are out there."

Buying the House

If you are interested in a home, make an offer. In an average market you can usually wheel and deal, but if the seller will not budge on the price, try to negotiate on other points. Tell the seller you will pay full price if he lets you keep all the appliances or if he will pay for the loan fee (which is usually 1–2 percent of the price of the home). Never just say you want the house. Try for that something extra. When those extras have been decided, include them in the contract and read the contract very carefully, making sure the seller will take care of any work orders that are needed. After you sign the contract, it's too late to make changes.

Now that the contract is signed, go back to your financial institution for the loan. Talk about the differences between Federal Housing Assistance (FHA) and conventional loans with your loan officer. FHA makes you pay a mortgage insurance reserve up front (which you get back when you sell the house), but you don't have to make as large a down payment.

Pete Shimer, the C.P.A., has several thoughts on

loans and payments: "Beware of Private Mortgage Insurance (PMI). PMI is only a protection for the bank in case you default on your loan. There is *no* benefit to you. PMI is a charge required by virtually all banks when they loan you more than 80 percent of the value of the home you are purchasing. Your monthly payments are increased by the PMI premium amount ($50–$100 per month average) until you have built at least 20 percent equity in your home. Avoid PMI if at all possible. This is where the gift from a relative is usually involved, to get you below the 80 percent loan amount.

"Investigate different financing options. Most banks will offer lower rates if the customer will take a variable rate loan (known as an ARM—Adjustable Rate Mortgage). ARM loan payments fluctuate over time based upon general interest rates. That can be good or bad depending on which way rates are going. Understand all the features of an ARM before buying, however. The hidden costs behind the low rate can be exorbitant! Ask the following questions:

- Is the initial rate just a teaser, which automatically gets adjusted early in the loan period?
- What index is the rate tied to and what is the spread (how much over the index)?
- Are there conversion features that allow you to lock into a fixed rate along the way, and if so, what are the costs of conversion?
- Is the loan assumable?
- What is the term of the loan? (Most fixed mortgages are thirty years.)
- Can you buy down the interest rate by paying points up front (basically prepaying interest to get a better loan rate)?
- Are taxes and insurance included in the monthly

payment? (If not, be sure to budget for them on a *monthly* basis.)

● Can you get a better rate by having your loan payment automatically deducted from your checking or saving account?

What's next?

Get your loan, sign the papers, wait for the sale to close, move into your home, and enjoy the privileges of being a home owner. Mow that lawn, fix that toilet, replace that carpet, repaint that bedroom—and wonder why you bought a home!

CHAPTER 16

The Ultimate Construction Project

In chapter 15, we discussed *buying* your home.

In this chapter, we're going to address *building* your home.

But the homes of chapters 15 and 16 are different. The home in this chapter is more important than the home in the previous one.

Listen to these words from the gospel of Matthew. Jesus is speaking to his disciples and to a crowd gathered to hear what was later called the Sermon on the Mount.

"Therefore everyone who hears these words of mine and puts them into practice is like a wise man who built his house on the rock. The rain came down, the streams rose, and the winds blew and beat against that house; yet it did not fall, because it had its foundation on the rock. But everyone who hears these words of mine and does not put them into practice is like a foolish man who built his house on sand. The rain came down, the streams rose, and the winds blew and beat against that house, and it fell with a great crash." (Matthew 7:24–27)

I think we have covered some important topics in this book. If I didn't think so, I probably wouldn't have wasted your time and my time writing about them.

We've talked about differences between college and life beyond college. We've learned about developmental tasks and about how to handle changing relationships, including friendships, roommates, marriage partners, children, and parents. We've looked at some practical suggestions for success in graduate school and the workplace. We've examined money and homes.

But, frankly, these themes are secondary to the subject of this chapter. Here we're dealing with the foundation for our lives.

With these words from Matthew, Jesus is wrapping up one of his most famous sermons. This is his closing statement. Previous to this point, he, too, has talked about relationships. He has given his audience advice on what to be looking for and what to do as they negotiate through life. But he wants to leave them with a word picture at the conclusion of his talk that will emphasize his key point and stick with them.

And so he talks about building houses. The wise man is careful of the foundation for his house. So he builds it on solid rock. The rains come, the stream rises, the winds blow and beat against the house, but it does not fall because the foundation is secure and firm.

In contrast to the wise person, there is the foolish man who builds his house on the sand. I wonder why? Was he lazy? Did it mean that he could get his house done faster and move to other items on his "to do" list? Did he build this foundation because he thought he was immune to storms?

In the end, of course, the rain came down, the streams rose, the winds blew and beat against that house, and it fell with a great crash.

What is the best foundation in life; what is that foundation of rock? I believe it is a relationship with Jesus Christ. Later in the book of Matthew, there is a conversation between Peter and Jesus. Jesus again uses the word picture of "rock" and says to Peter, "And I tell you that you are Peter, and on this rock I will build my church" (Matthew 16:18).

What is the rock to which Jesus refers? I believe that rock is the confession that Peter makes in verse 16. Jesus has just asked Peter, "But what about you? Who do you say I am?" And Peter replies, "You are the Christ, the Son of the living God."

Peter is saying, in essence, "You, Jesus, are the Messiah, the Savior, the person we've been waiting for. You are the person who will cleanse us from sin and renew a right spirit within us. You are the way, the truth, and the life. Everything you've said about yourself and about life is true. I am willing to bet my life on you."

The church will be built on this belief. Jesus is the rock. And to tie Matthew 7 to Matthew 16, Jesus is the foundation on which our house should be built if we are going to withstand the storms of life.

And there are storms. No one is immune. Relationships fail. Economic situations change. Corporate raiders buy up your parent company and suddenly you're unemployed. Life is untidy and it doesn't always turn out like our plans say it should.

But when the rains come and the streams rise and the winds beat against your very life, you have the security of realizing that your foundation is solid both now and for eternal life.

A Piece of the Rock

How do we go about establishing that foundation?

Step one is to acknowledge your dependence on Jesus Christ. We must say along with Peter, "You are the Christ." We must admit our need for him, acknowledge that we have sinned, and acknowledge that he is our solution. We need to pledge our allegiance and our life to the Lord Jesus Christ.

Step two is to grow in that relationship. Like any human relationship, this relationship with Christ will take time and effort. In chapter 5, some twentysomething people gave some points and principles for developing human relationships. Let's do the same for this most important, *foundational* relationship, the relationship with Jesus Christ himself.

1. *Communication is crucial.* The basis for any relationship is communication. With Jesus, that communication takes the form of prayer. Prayer is simply talking to God, telling him what's on your mind, telling him how much you appreciate him, and asking him for help for you and others. Prayer is also listening—pausing and thinking and letting God speak to you. For myself, I don't hear the audible voice of God. I never have. But I do get what I call "hunches"—thoughts about how he would want me to approach a task, a challenge, a situation, a person.

The other part of communication besides prayer is reading the Bible. I like to think of the Bible as a personal letter to me to help me know Jesus better and what he has in mind for me. If a friend were to send you letters and you never opened them, your relationship would suffer. I see the Bible as a letter from my best friend and also from my commander-in-chief. I need to open that letter and read it.

Bob Regan also has some thoughts on why we should read Scripture. "I believe you can't demonstrate that which you don't understand, for our actions are the result of what we understand. Discipleship, as Christ demonstrated, should begin with understanding the nature, qualities, and character of God. We often emphasize ordering our actions to come in line with our belief structure. The problem, of course, is many people don't *understand* what they believe. Understanding means to comprehend, to grasp the nature, significance, or explanation of something."

So we also read the Word to better understand what it is we really believe and who it is we really trust.

2. *Hanging out with like-minded people and encouraging one another is important to building one's foundations.* In Christian communities, that type of hanging out is called "fellowship." Both time and commitment are important for strong Christian fellowship. Time is needed because time is crucial to the development of a committed relationship (remember the time/commitment/communication diagram of chapter 6?). And commitment is needed because people need to be dedicated to holding each other accountable and to helping each other along. The writer of the book of Hebrews describes this type of fellowship: "And let us consider how we may spur one another on toward love and good deeds. Let us not give up meeting together, as some are in the habit of doing, but let us encourage one another—and all the more as you see the Day approaching" (Hebrews 10:24–25).

Part of this fellowship should include worship, as you and your fellow Christians praise and thank God for who he is and what he has done. The older I become, the more convinced I am of the importance of worship, because it reminds us weekly of the greatness of God and our dependence on him.

Part of this fellowship can also center around small groups of six to ten people who meet regularly to check in with each other, to study the Bible, to pray together, and once in awhile, to serve together in ministry. I am a firm believer in the importance of small groups while you're in college and beyond.

3. *Being obedient to Christ is foundational.* In the parable of the wise and foolish builders, Jesus said, "But everyone who hears these words of mine and does not put them into practice is like a foolish man who built his house on sand" (Matthew 7:26). Obedience is crucial for two reasons. It keeps us out of a lot of trouble. I am convinced you do "reap what you sow."

But it also helps us to be a player in God's design for this world. As we are obedient to him and reach out to share our faith with others, we become part of God's team. There is joy in serving Christ in the midst of the rain, the flooding streams, and the winds that beat against you in your twenties and beyond.

CHAPTER 17

Is Success a Moving Target?

Is Mother Teresa successful?
Donald Trump?
Joe Montana?
George Bush?
Gretha Osterberg? (You've never heard of Gretha? She's one of my heroes—a wonderful mom, grandmother, and church administrative assistant.)

Are you successful? Can you be successful at twenty-something? Or do you have to wait?

How do you measure success? Is it a moving target, an elusive something that you never know if you have? Is success based on the amount of money one makes, the power one wields, the position one holds, or the satisfaction one derives from a job well done? Is it all of the above? Or none? Or is there more to success?

As we conclude this book, I'd like to share a few principles and a few suggestions regarding that subject that concerns most of us: success. Let's begin by considering Peggy. She's made her living as a bicycle messenger shuttling packages and correspondence across town. After knowing her occupation, how would you rate her on your success meter?

I should also tell you that Peggy is one of the two

American women ever to have stood atop the highest peak in the world, Mount Everest.

With very limited mountain-climbing experience, Peggy joined a team of climbers whose goal was to place the very first American woman on the top of the mountain. Of the ten who teamed up on the trip, three were women. Three of the party made it to the top. Two of them were women. One of them was Peggy. She has a place in history. Where does that rate on the success meter?

Or take Dan Ibabao, the sound engineer. Here's what Dan says, "I carry a video deck and microphones for a living. My ears are my livelihood. The pay is crummy and the hours are long. But I think I'm successful. I've traveled to Australia, Denmark, France, Guatemala, Norway, Puerto Rico, Japan, Hong Kong, Sweden, St. Thomas, St. Croix, and right now I'm writing this passage while on assignment on the island of Martinique. I've won three Emmy Awards for my audio work and have contributed work on countless other award-winning projects. As one of my colleagues says, 'You could be working for a living.'

"I believe that success, like beauty, is totally subjective, a personal thing. You may be the best judge of your own success. Sure, others will judge you, but it will be according to their standards. Have confidence in yourself and truly do the best you can. Go out and have a good time in whatever job you're doing. You'll be a success."

And then there are the people who even have names that declare them a success. Consider my friend named, appropriately, Mike Champion. He says, "It would probably be pretty easy for others to view me as a success. I have won awards, I have played professional basketball, my net worth is very good, and I have a wonderful and beautiful wife. Yet it is only when I have allowed God to completely control my life that I have felt truly successful. Real success stems from the relationship between a believer and God."

Stu Harris says, "During your twenties there are a myriad of changes. Many times family and friends (or even you yourself) have very high expectations for you to achieve. Achievement is a good thing. Just keep in mind God's scale of success and failure. Don't sacrifice his view to please family or anybody.

"During your twenties, you will 'try' many things. Failure will come, but don't let that keep you from taking risks. The risks are what makes it exciting.

"I was recently talking with my wife, Sue, before New Year's. We were sharing our 'highlights of the eighties.' Among other things, I listed being fired from my first career job. Though it was a very difficult thing at the time, it turned out to be one of the best things that happened to me. I now find myself not only in a job suited particularly to me, but with a better understanding of God's grace and will for my life. This 'failure' in the eyes of the world was part of God's successful plan to bring me closer to him."

I wanted to end this book with the story of Peggy and the comments of Dan and Mike and Stu because I feel that they've got a handle on success that is important as you move beyond college. Success isn't in the money that you make, the job that you have, the way that you look, the car that you drive, the beauty of the person to whom you're married, the awards that you've achieved. Because then success does become a moving target.

Instead success must be found in something consistent and attainable, something that can sustain satisfaction. Jesus said, "I am come that they may have life, and have it to the full" (John 10:10). Defining success must begin first and foremost on a spiritual level. A relationship with Jesus Christ gives us an unmovable source of acceptance, love, and strength that enables us to face changes, failures, and the pressures of society. If you only step away with one thought from this book, I hope it will be this: *success is found in a personal relationship with Jesus Christ*. Otherwise success is a moving target. Standards change and feelings fade. But Christ is consistent, unchanging, solid.

And that's good news with which to end this book.

CONTRIBUTORS

I want to thank my twenty-six friends who contributed to this book. This writing project was one of collaboration, and I'm grateful to them and to my family for their creative support and encouragement.

Jim Allen graduated in 1987 from the University of Washington with a degree in psychology. After spending a year as a missionary in Africa at the University of Jos in Nigeria, he spent one year as a University Ministries intern at University Presbyterian Church in Seattle. He is now a student at Fuller Theological Seminary in Pasadena, California. He will be getting married next spring.

Bruce Bailey is the quintessential entrepreneur, a creator who has successfully dabbled in graphics, design, and restaurant and real estate development. He and his wife, Gay, have been married for thirty years and have two daughters and four grandchildren. Bruce is also a talented tennis player and golfer, but spends most of his time hanging out with college students.

Steve and Lisa Call have been married four years and have a young son, Jordan, who will soon celebrate his first birthday. Steve graduated from the University of Washington in 1986 with a degree in economics. He has since worked as the missions coordinator for the college ministry at University Presbyterian Church. Lisa also graduated from the University of Washington. She works part-time with troubled children and part-time as an aerobics instructor.

Mike Champion is a 6'9", 235-pound former professional basketball player who has played for the Seattle Supersonics and for an Australian team. He graduated from Gonzaga University with a degree in finance and a minor in economics. He and his wife, Lindsey, were married in the summer of 1989. They now live in San Diego, where Mike is in commercial real estate and Lindsey is a nurse.

Doug Early in the last four years has graduated from the University of Washington with a degree in English literature; taught English in China; studied theology for a year at Regent College in Vancouver, Canada; and become engaged to Andrea Campbell, whom he'll marry this summer.

Jim and Lisa Francese currently live in Yorba Linda, California. Jim has degrees in chemical engineering from Cornell University and the University of Washington. Lisa has a degree in nutrition from Cornell and is currently a nursing student at Azusa Pacific University. They have been married three years and enjoy sports, traveling, and camping.

Ken Green received his B.A. and M.A. in speech communications from the University of Washington. He is currently a part-time faculty member at Seattle Central Community College and a contract trainer for the Boeing Company. Ken is an avid volleyball player.

Doug Hansen is a psychiatric social worker in private practice in Seattle. What he knows about adult development comes from the books he reads, the clients he sees, and personal experience.

Stu and Sue Harris were married in July of 1988. Both served as University Ministries interns at University Presbyterian Church in Seattle after graduating from the University of Washington. In 1989, they moved to Japan, where they have been teaching English and enjoying the adventure of learning in another culture.

Dan Ibabao works for a television station in Seattle. His most memorable moment? Sharing personal space with a mountain gorilla, while on location. When he's not carrying his microphones, Dan likes to travel, play volleyball, and collect baseball cards. Dan came to Christ a few years ago on April 15th, the day taxes are due!

Pat Kelly graduated from the University of Washington with a degree in English in 1990. After a summer of traveling and mission work, he accepted a position as a youth director at a church in Seattle. When he's not being terrorized by his youth group, he loves writing, reading, sports, and country music.

156

Eric and Lisa Kragerud have been married since 1986 and are expecting their first child. Lisa graduated from Washington State University, then served as a University Ministries intern at University Presbyterian Church in Seattle. Eric graduated from the University of Washington. Lisa is a junior high youth director

and Eric is a sales representative. They enjoy traveling, singing, and pickleball. In their spare time they buy older homes and fix them up.

Mark and Virginia Larson are the parents of two children, Luke and Mallory, and have been married ten years. Mark graduated from Florida State University with a criminology degree and from the University of Puget Sound

with a law degree. He is currently serving as senior deputy prosecuting attorney for King County, Washington. He enjoys basketball and bicycling. Virginia attended Pepperdine University, then graduated from Florida State with a degree in sociology. She worked with Merrill Lynch before devoting her time to raising their children. She is an avid gardener, creative decorator, and great conversationalist.

Peter Larson is Mark's big brother, and pastor of First Presbyterian Church of Garden Grove, California. Before entering the ministry, Peter worked for ten years as a newspaper reporter in Florida and Texas. The turning point in his life came in 1983 when he joined a church in Texas and encountered the love and forgiveness of Jesus Christ. He holds a journalism

degree from Northwestern University and a master of divinity degree from Princeton Seminary. Peter and his wife, Elizabeth, have a baby daughter, Abigail.

Kelly Lunda graduated from the University of Wisconsin in 1987 with a degree in physical therapy. She is a former National Speedskating Champion and is still very active in athletics and in the Fellowship of Christian Athletes. She now lives in Seattle.

Mike Neelley is presently the director of junior high ministries at University Presbyterian Church in Seattle. He is a graduate of the University of Washington with a degree in English. He is an avid volleyball player, and he writes and publishes poetry.

Bob and Tracy Regan are both University of Washington graduates. Bob is in the business of acquiring, developing, and managing commercial-grade apartments. Tracy spends a great deal of her time with their two young daughters. While in college, both Bob and Tracy were involved in summer missions. Bob served in inner-city Washington D.C., and Tracy ministered in Austria.

Denny Rydberg graduated from Seattle Pacific University in 1967 with a B.A. in psychology. He did graduate work at Western Washington University. He has served as a youth director, Christian education director, magazine editor, company vice president, and director of operations and consultant for a film company. He is also the author of *Beyond Graduation* and *How to Survive in College*.

Marilyn Rydberg graduated from the University of Oregon with a degree in sociology and then served with Campus Crusade for eleven years. She and Denny are the directors of University Ministries at University Presbyterian Church in Seattle. They have four children—Heather, Joshua, Jeremy, and Jonathan.

Pete Shimer is a senior manager at the public accounting firm of Deloitte and Touche. He graduated from the University of Washington, where he was "the slowest man ever to play for the Husky basketball team." He is married to Laurel and they are expecting their first child.

159

Tim and Carroll Snow have been married eleven years and have two girls, Kendall and Annie. Tim is pastor of congregational development at University Presbyterian Church in Seattle. Carroll is an occupational therapist at Virginia Mason Hospital. Tim graduated from San Jose State and Fuller Theological Seminary. Carroll is a University of Washington graduate. Tim is a tennis player and sailing buff, and Carroll loves to travel.